Beyond the "Clobber" Passages

Rethinking Homosexuality & the Bible

Copyright Information

BEYOND THE "CLOBBER" PASSAGES
Rethinking Homosexuality & the Bible

Table of Contents

INTRODUCTION

"There's a mighty wind's a'blowin..."[1]

A shift is happening among many thousands (perhaps millions?) of dedicated Christ-followers today. While they passionately love Jesus and respect the Bible, some things that once made sense are no longer spiritually or intellectually satisfying. Concepts, convictions, and certainties that were once firmly held start to feel like they are slowly eroding. This is disconcerting to the one experiencing it, especially if one is naturally averse to change.

One's spiritual support group (aka their local church) is often reactionary. This is especially true the more forceful and dogmatic the leaders and the members are.

Those who are experiencing this process may worry that they are giving in to 'sinful' doubt, or 'compromising with the world', backsliding, or even purchasing a fast trip to hell. Reactions from others can range from apprehensive concern ("I'll pray for you to get over your doubts") to blaming the devil ("you need to resist the spirit of doubt!") to exhortations and warnings about falling away from 'biblical' teachings.

---

[1] From the 2003 Christopher Guest movie *"A Mighty Wind"*

In some churches, there can be a very strong current that makes it hard for a person to swim upstream. It seems that a person faces three options when in that situation: suppress their intuitions and flow with the current by following the majority downstream, continue resisting because they find swimming against the current rewarding, or get out of the water – leave the situation entirely.

Tough choices.

A Flashback

This is not the first time in our collective history that the Church[2] has had to grapple with controversial issues and rethink some beliefs, practices, and attitudes that had been considered "the way things always have been," including scriptural interpretations, cultural assumptions, and certain practices.

For instance, in the early 50s CE, when large numbers of non-Jewish people (called Gentiles) began to embrace belief in a Jewish Messiah named Jesus, there was great controversy over whether the Gentiles must first become Jews by submitting to Jewish practices such as male circumcision, as required in the Jewish Bible, to become a Christ-follower. After a rather contentious church council of

[2] In this book, when "Church" is capitalized, I am referring to either a) the universal church that embodies Christianity, or b) a large group of Christians such as the American Church.

apostles and leaders (see Acts 15 for details) it was determined that Gentiles did not need to be circumcised to follow Christ. Contemporary readers might question the significance of this matter, but within the historical context and cultural framework of that era, it was of considerable importance. Those decisions changed the trajectory of the Church forever.

Another instance, much closer to our day, was the issue of slavery in America in the early-mid 1800s. Historian Mark Knoll traces the deep theological divide between Christians in the southern United States and those in the north (though there were a few exceptions on each side.)[3] Ironically, the southern Christians had a distinct abundance of biblical "proof" in both the Old and New Testaments that slavery was a God-endorsed institution.

Yet they were wrong.

Historian and writer Phyllis Tickle has noted that around every 500 years the Church has a "rummage sale," discarding some old ways of beliefs and practices and embracing new ones.[4] Each "sale" produced monumental changes:

---

[3] See Knoll, Mark, *The Civil War as a Theological Crisis* (Raleigh: The University of North Carolina Press, 2015)

[4] For a fascinating study of this topic, I highly recommend Phyllis Tickle's book *The Great Emergence* (Grand Rapids, MI: Baker Books, 2008). Available from Amazon here: The Great Emergence: How Christianity Is Changing and Why (Emergent Village Resources for Communities of Faith): Phyllis Tickle: 9780801013133: Amazon.com: Books

- @500 – 600 CE – Pope Gregory I (also called Pope Gregory the Great.) By the time Gregory became the leader of the worldwide Church, Rome and its empire had been destroyed by invaders from the north. Many of the invaders settled in Rome, adopted Christianity, and then blended it with spiritism and pagan practices. Gregory was instrumental in developing the monastic system – monasteries and convents were established throughout Europe. While many modern protestants look askance as those institutions, the reality is that those institutions, while not perfect, protected the sacred doctrines of Christianity which protestants cherish today, not to mention such important items as literacy and scripture. Gregory also became a strong reformer and innovator of Christian music. (Ever hear of "Gregorian Chants?" Those were the contemporary Christian music of that day!)
- 1044 CE – The Great Schism: the final official split between Roman Catholicism, Eastern Orthodox, and the Coptic Church (eastern Africa), the great pillars of the Christian faith. The reasons are too many and too complicated to discuss here, though most moderns would consider those reasons (at

least the theological ones) as quibbling. A thousand years later, it is still not resolved. (One wonders if many of the controversial issues that divide us now will seem like quibbling to our descendants in 500 years, but I digress.)

- @1500 CE – the Protestant Reformation, with famous names such as Martin Luther, John Calvin, and John Wycliffe. They rejected some of the practices and beliefs of the Roman Catholic church, and their reforms and theologies are still influential to this day.
- @2000 and beyond – we are still in the birthing process, but many alterations and adjustments are developing.

The irony is that, despite the great differences in interpretation and emphases, Christians in all the above examples used the *same* Bible to defend their cherished positions, often denouncing and excommunicating those with whom they disagreed. This perspective seems inherent in most groups – a tragic part of our spiritual DNA.

It Works Until It Doesn't

My favorite phrase these days is "It works until it doesn't." It is disconcerting to many that a cherished belief or teaching that they once held dear, that nourished them emotionally, intellectually, and spiritually, now has lost its impact and feels dull and stale.

Like a balloon emptied of air.

Or the bubbly fizz gone from your favorite drink.

I have gradually learned that this is often the Spirit of God causing this sense of dissatisfaction, trying to gently lead us into something better, healthier, and always toward more love for God and others. The Bible describes this as the Spirit leading us "from glory to glory."[5] Though unsettling at times, it is still a wonderful, adventurous process that improves our lives and strengthens our spirituality.

Think of this process as a house remodel. The house may have been a fine building at the beginning, but now not so much. Sometimes an old house or one that was poorly constructed needs everything reestablished – from the foundation to the wall studs to the joists above the ceiling. It may need plumbing and electrical replacements. Some rooms may be enlarged, while other rooms disappear altogether. Ironically, sometimes previous remodeling projects need an updated remodel themselves.

Sometimes the remodel may be less ambitious: replacing old plaster walls with drywall; a new tub and shower; new kitchen cupboards; new light fixtures, flooring, and wall colors.

---

[5] 2 Corinthians 3:18 (King James Version)

Whether we know it or not, our lives are like naïve homeowners who have just bought a major "fixer upper!" We do not fully know how much remodeling we will need. Only the Master Contractor knows. And in his kindness and patience, if we let him, he will remodel continually yet gently:

In some cases, the upgrade may primarily involve aesthetic enhancements, such as fresh paint and an updated tile backsplash in the kitchen.

Sometimes the upgrade will be more substantial, such as an updated bathroom, or eliminating mold from the basement

Sometimes the upgrade will be major: include restoring crumbling foundations or a complete rewiring of the house to get it up to code.

But eventually the house will become solid, safe, and beautiful.

So, Why This Book?

One of the major controversies in the Church in our time is the issue of homosexuality. In case some of my readers are not familiar with the issues from a conservative Christian perspective, I have boiled them down to eight questions that conservative Christians (whether protestant or Catholic) struggle with:

- Is homosexuality a sin?

- Does God hate homosexuals, or at least homosexual activity?
- Is homosexuality simply a learned behavior (a choice) or is it innate (born with it)?
- Can someone be gay and still be a Christian?
- Does a gay person have to be celibate to be a Christian?
- Does God recognize and bless gay marriage?
- Should gay couples be allowed to adopt children?
- Can a gay person serve in leadership in a local church? What if he/she is celibate?

Trying to address all these questions is beyond the scope of this book. However, if we can get a grasp on the first three questions, I believe the rest of the questions will be resolved.

Astute readers may have already guessed what my conclusions will be. If you are a Christ-follower, you may have had intuitions that what you have been taught about this issue may not reflect our heavenly Father's heart. Yet you want to remain loyal to scripture. If you are struggling with this, then this book was written for you.

If you are part of the LGBTQ+ community and are reading this, I hope you will stick with me and read to the end. The ideas will encourage and enrich your life.

If you, my dear reader, strongly disagree with me, I respect that you do so out of our shared love and commitment to Christ and to scripture. I do hope you will thoughtfully, humbly, and prayerfully consider what I have to say.

So, let's begin!

CHAPTER 1 – Party with a Billionaire

Once upon a time not so long ago....

There was an extremely wealthy man who was also known for his kindness and generosity. One day he received the wonderful news that he had been named at the top of Forbes's 400 list of richest people in the world! He decided to celebrate and invite all his friends and business associates to a great banquet at his palatial estate. He had his assistants send out the invitations along with an RSVP request by email.

In a short time, the responses came in – but most of them were extremely disappointing. Here are some samples:

"Congrats on topping the Forbes 400 list! Also, thanks for the invitation. Unfortunately, we have scheduled the maiden voyage of our new yacht later that week, so we need time to pack. Ciao!"

Another one:

"I appreciate you including me for this festive occasion. However, I am entertaining some business clients that night in my stadium suite at the football game."

Another one:

"You know I would love to attend your wonderful event, but my wife and I will have just returned from a long overseas flight a couple of days before and will probably have jet lag."

As the RSVPs followed one another, the world's wealthiest man was at first disappointed, but then became increasingly angry. Had he not helped these people in the past, he reasoned? Had they not called him their best friend for the money he gave them or loaned them at zero per cent interest? Was this the way they showed their gratefulness?

He decided, however, that the banquet was still going to happen. But who could he invite? Why not people in the community who were middle or lower-middle class who had never been to such a grand festivity? His estate's ballroom alone could handle a large throng, and the massive rooms throughout the mansion as well as the meticulously manicured lawns could accommodate any overflow.

The gentleman called his assistants to his office and said, "Go to the county clerk's office, get a computer printout of all the homeowners in the city and invite them. Then, locate all the apartment buildings, learn the names of the renters, and send invitations to them as well!" His assistants were stunned, not only at his generosity, but over the concern of how they would be able to locate all that information. Seeing their confused looks, he stared at them for a moment and then said, "I hired you because you know how to manage large amounts of data. Figure it out! Go do it now!" And with that, his assistants quickly exited his office to do the herculean task.

Two weeks later, they returned to his office to report that, indeed, they had been successful, and there were hundreds of people who sent RSVPs stating they would attend.

"But there is a problem," explained his top assistant. "According to our calculations, even if everyone who RSVP'd shows up, your place is so big that it will still only seem half full. What do you suggest we do now?"

The wealthy man thought for a moment, and then a smile broke across his face. He declared, "I have a great idea! No one would expect this, but I think it's brilliant! Here is who I want you to invite," and he began to list the type of people who would never be invited to a celebration given by the world's richest man. He continued, "Invite every person who our local society wouldn't want to eat with! I don't care who they are: prostitutes, drug dealers, gang members, mobsters, pimps, thieves, anyone with a criminal record – invite them to the banquet! Oh, and we have a couple areas in the city that have homeless encampments. Invite those people as well! This is going to be one spectacular, bodacious, amazing, fantastic, blow-out experience for all of them."

His assistants were shocked and even appalled by some of the individuals on that new invitation list. However, they could feel their boss's excitement as well as sense his steely determination. They knew better than to try to discourage him from inviting some of the 'less-desirable' people in their community. So, the invitations were sent.

The response of that last group of people invited was fascinating. Hardly anyone responded with the RSVP. This group knew they were not accepted by the establishment and thought the invitations were at best a scam or at worst a plot to arrest them. Perhaps this was an undercover sting operation. Since many in that group had outstanding warrants for their arrest, or were known to regularly commit criminal acts, maybe the police would show up and take them all into custody. Even though many of them secretly wanted to experience such a lavish party for themselves, it was probably not worth the risk. Some also figured that, even if they went, they would be served a cheap hamburger and fries from some burger joint while the "beautiful people" would have filet mignon and expensive wine.

The wealthy man's employees soon realized that, of all the RSVPs that had been received, almost none came from that group of 'undesirables.' Upon further research they learned the kind of fears that were keeping that last group from attending the party. The employees also knew that their boss expected a packed house for his party. Their only option was to fan out across the city to convince any they could find that yes, this was a legitimate invitation to a celebration and no, it was not a mistake they were invited. It seemed almost as though they had to drag some of them to the feast.

However, the world's richest man was right.

That party was indeed a massive blowout celebration – outstanding food and top-shelf wine for all, a fantastic dance band, and merriment throughout the mansion. It was the talk of the town for years to come.

Hopefully this story sparks recognition for my readers.

Let's discuss its implications...

CHAPTER 2 – The Story Behind the Story

The party story in chapter 1 is an update of one that Jesus told in the Gospel of Luke, chapter 14. In context, Jesus was describing something he called "the kingdom of God" or "the kingdom of heaven." Contrary to what many believe, his stories about the kingdom had nothing to do with the afterlife.[6] Most of the time, when Jesus taught about a kingdom, it had to do with the here-and-now, not the "sweet by-and by".

How do we know this?

First, when Jesus described the kingdom in stories or sayings, most times he used the present tense. It was always said "the kingdom of heaven *IS* like...", not "the kingdom of heaven *will someday* be like..."

Second, most of his stories or sayings make no sense if applied to the afterlife:

- The kingdom of heaven is like mustard seed...
- The kingdom of heaven is like yeast put in bread dough...
- The kingdom of heaven is like finding a treasure in a field...

---

[6] "Kingdom of heaven" was a euphemism for "kingdom of God." The term was used mostly in Matthew's gospel because of sensitivities some of his readers had as they had been taught not to say the word "God" lest they misuse and break one of the Ten Commandments (not taking the Lord's name in vain).

- The kingdom of heaven is like a rare, expensive pearl...
- The kingdom of heaven is like seeds scattered on various types of soil...

There are many more, but I think my readers will get the picture. None of the word pictures above make any sense if Jesus was talking about heavenly bliss in the afterlife.

Third, for those in Jesus' day who believed in an afterlife, the common assumption was resurrection of the human body at the end of time (rather than going to heaven when they died.) Even then, most of the religious elite (like the Sadducees) did not even believe in an afterlife, and especially not a bodily resurrection. For Jesus to talk about going to a place called heaven at death would have made no sense to the people who listened to him.

Fourth, most of the time when Jesus talked about the kingdom, he described it as "near," "among you," or "in you." In other words, a present reality in which all had access if they wanted it.

So, what is the Kingdom of Heaven?

Since most 21st century North Americans don't use the term "kingdom" in any significant way, perhaps there are better terminologies that could be used:

- *Reign of God.* A realm in which God is in charge and human beings and their systems are not. It means conforming our values to the teachings, values, and example of Christ and how to live those out in our lives.
- *Commonwealth of God.* Think of the British Commonwealth in the 19th century; the phrase "the sun never sets on the British flag" meant that the rule of Britian and its monarchs reached around the globe. The Commonwealth of God encompasses the whole earth wherever people are following Christ and his teachings and enacting his example with others. Perhaps this was alluded to in the words of one of the world's most famous prayers, when Jesus prayed, "Your kingdom come, your will be done *on earth* as it is in heaven." As someone once said, "Heaven is just fine – it's down here where the problems are!"
- *Community of God.* Like the Commonwealth of God but implies more of a relational connection with others.
- St. Paul described God's kingdom as *justice, peace, and joy in the Holy Spirit.*[7] In other words, where those exist, the kingdom is there.

---

[7] Romans 14:17

So again, what is this all about?

In chapter one, the story of the party was a description of the banqueting atmosphere of the kingdom of God. While many hope that someday in the afterlife there will be such an event (and who knows, there may be), its most effective meaning has to do with the desire, heart, and will of God for us *now*.

Everyone (and I mean *everyone*) is invited to the celebration.

Some refuse, notably those regarded as mutual "friends" of themselves and the rich man.

Others who never thought they would have qualified for a grand celebration like that discover that they are indeed invited, even though they have no previous connection with the wealthy gentleman.

People who were the outcasts (homeless, morally challenged, thugs, etc.) are welcomed and treated as if they are longtime friends of the world's richest man.

This is the image of what the kingdom, reign, commonwealth, and community of God is like! And this is the picture of what God is like according to Jesus, who knew God better than anyone. Which brings us to the foundational concept we must face – in the deepest recesses of your heart, what is your image of God?

CHAPTER 3 – Does Your God Love a Party?

Thou shalt not make unto thee any graven image...[8]

Everyone has an image of God.

Each religion teaches that God—-by whatever name they refer to—-has certain characteristics that describe how they understand the Divine. Ironically, even atheists have an image of the God in whom they do not believe. While an agnostic may honestly say that she has no personal knowledge of a deity and thus no opinion, if asked what she would expect a deity to be like if one existed, she could probably provide a description. Hence, an image of God appears.

Raised in a strong Christian environment as a preacher's kid, and later spending many years in ministry, I have observed many images of God. From the most conservative fundamentalist to the most progressive mainline denomination, every church emphasizes a particular image of God.

So... I am going to address my Christian brothers and sisters. This is not a private conversation, and if you, my dear reader, do not identify as a Christian, you are welcome to continue

---

[8] Exodus 20:4 (King James Version)

reading, as you may track quite well with what I am about to say.

If I asked my many friends who are fundamentalist, evangelical, or charismatic to describe their image of God, the response from many of them would be something like, "Well, I see God as how he's described in the Bible." Some of them may instead give an answer using adjectives that describe God as loving, holy, just, powerful, etc. Then the question becomes, "On what do you base those descriptions?" The response will almost always be, "That's what the Bible teaches," or "That's what I learned from my pastor (or a particular theologian I read.)"

This demonstrates a significant problem that most Christians have never thought about, and if they have, they either choose to ignore it or try to make everything fit.

The issue is that there is not just one image of God in the Bible. There are several images, and some are contradictory!

Think about it.

The Bible did not drop out of heaven fully formed as one big book. It is a collection, a library if you will, of 66 individual books[9] that were written over a thousand-year period in three ancient languages and rooted in different cultures. I am writing the book you are reading in 2025. Imagine going back

_____

[9] More if one uses the Catholic, Orthodox, or some Anglican editions.

one thousand years to 1025 CE. If you were in Europe, what would it be like? This would be almost 300 years *before* the Bubonic plague ravaged Europe and Asia; 430 years before the invention of the printing press; 400 years before many of the famous explorers sailed for a new world, 500 years before Shakespeare; 752 years before the Declaration of Independence was signed.

A lot of things will change in a thousand years!

A thousand years ago, people believed the sun revolved around a flat earth. Kings had absolute authority and insisted that they had a divine right given them by God to rule however they saw fit. The concept of feudal lords owning the land was taking hold across the continent of Europe. The lord would provide protection and meager wages to peasants who would work the land for him – something akin to modern sharecroppers.

Medicine was antiquated. Lifespans tended to be much shorter. Science was in its infancy. Technology as we know it was quite primitive. Illiteracy, poverty, and disease were the norm for most people.

Most people believed that weather and other natural disasters were caused by God (or the gods – depending on one's belief system.) In their assessment, droughts, floods, bad storms, earthquakes, volcanoes were all caused by a deity who was either angry with them or at least indifferent.

Now, take this concept of changes over a thousand-year-period back to the time when the Bible was written (approximately 1000 BCE – 100 CE). Different authors had different images of God, and this came out in their writings. As I detailed in my book *A More Beautiful Faith*,[10] there are indications that early authors saw Yahweh as their tribal god who defended them when they were obedient and punished them with famine, war, poverty, or sickness when they disobeyed. Later they viewed Yahweh as one of many gods who existed but who was the greatest and strongest.[11]

> *Great is the LORD! He is most worthy of praise!*
> *He is to be feared above all gods.*[12]

Later the concept developed that there was only one real God – Yahweh – and all the other 'gods' were merely the inventions of humans. Yahweh was viewed as the God who rules all heaven and earth.

Along with this theological evolution that took place over a thousand years, the characteristics ascribed to God changed. In the earliest biblical stories, it seems that the characters' experiences

---

[10] Brown, Dennis, *A More Beautiful Faith – Seeing God Through the Eyes of Jesus*, (Knoxville: Metanoia Publishers LLC), chapter 12. Available on Amazon.
[11] The term for this is "monolatry" – many gods but we just worship one.
[12] Psalm 96:4, for example

with God were relational: God walking with Adam and Eve in the garden, even kindly making clothes for them after they disobeyed. God's interaction with Cain and Abel, even providing protection for Cain after he murdered his brother. God's interaction and protection for Noah. God's closeness with Enoch. The dynamic experiences that Abraham, Isaac, and Jacob had with Yahweh. God even called Abraham his friend.

"*Everyone* has an image of God."

However, the biblical writers' views of God evolved (or perhaps devolved) to become more transactional. It became for most people an "if/then" scenario. Scripture says that God had a close relationship with Moses, speaking "face to face."[13] Sadly, the beauty of that relationship was instead overshadowed by Moses's laws to the Israelites.[14]

According to the Bible, God gave Moses divine lists of blessings and curses based on obedience (with the list of curses for disobedience twice as long

---

[13] Deuteronomy 34:10 *et al.*

[14] I acknowledge that many modern Old Testament scholars have concluded that those writings were either written hundreds of years after Moses (during the time of King David), or were at least greatly edited, added to, or abridged during that later period. Be that as it may, my main point still stands regarding a transactional Deity.

as the blessings list).[15] The image was a deity that could be kind and generous but extremely wrathful if crossed — much like the images of the absolute rulers of the day.

Unfortunately, for many Christians in our time, this is still the dominant inner image they have of God, even if they know the right buzz words of 'grace' and 'love'. I have known many people who, if they were more deeply self-aware, would not perceive God as the one who throws a great party for all. A better and more honest depiction would be God as a party-pooper!

Intertwined with that image is confusion over "cause and effect."

Let me explain.

It seems the universe is set up for cause and effect. The earth's rotation and current position of the moon affect the ocean tides. Tectonic plates shift and there is an earthquake. Tornadoes occur due to rapid temperature changes combined with specific storm patterns.

None of these are considered acts done by God.

Except, of course, for insurance companies, who suddenly become expert theologians when a natural disaster hits: "Oh, I'm sorry, we can't cover this since it was an act of God. It's right there in your policy."

But I digress.

---

[15] Deuteronomy 28

Most agree that our actions trigger cause-and-effect (CAE) scenarios. The question is whether this suggests a transactional God or natural CAE. For example:

- A woman smokes three packs of cigarettes a day for thirty years and then develops lung cancer. Is the cancer the result of God's punishment or simply an unhealthy habit?
- A morbidly obese man doesn't diet or exercise and develops diabetes, high blood pressure, and heart issues. Are those health issues God's retribution or simply the results of poor choices?
- Due to over-ambition and a pathological desire to succeed, a young man does whatever it takes to become a wealthy leader in his profession, even sacrificing the relationships toward his wife and children. He pursued what he truly valued, but now his wife has remarried, and his children are permanently estranged. God or CAE?
- A 25-year-old is involved in several promiscuous sexual relationships. An unwanted pregnancy and sexually transmitted diseases result. God's punishment or poor choices?
- In the 1980s and early 1990s, HIV/AIDS decimated the gay population due to sexual encounters in bath houses, clubs, and other

venues. Prominent preachers proclaimed this as God's vengeance on homosexuals, and many Christians concurred. This is *exhibit "A"* of the image of a transactional God.

Some may ask, "Why can't it be both God and CAE? Maybe God is using CAE to punish those who are disobedient!"

Without the arrival of the most important person in history, perhaps such a case, based on certain Bible verses, could be made.

But when Jesus enters, the image of a transactional God is shattered!

His view of his heavenly Father flew in the face of the common views of the transactional God held by the people of his day. Notice how Jesus describes God:

> *"You have heard the law that says, 'Love your neighbor' and hate your enemy. But I say, **love your enemies**! Pray for those who persecute you! **In that way, you will be acting as true children of your Father in heaven. For he gives his sunlight to both the evil and the good, and he sends rain on the just and the unjust alike.**"* [16] [Emphasis mine]

---

[16] Matthew 5:43-45

According to Jesus, his Father's love and care for creation is universal – he feeds the birds, adorns the flowers, and cares for all of us.[17] He corrected his followers when they assumed that the cause of a man to be born blind was either sin committed by his parents or by the fetus itself![18] He punctured the pious egos of those who thought the fatalities from recent disasters were because the victims were 'sinners' who deserved such punishment from God.[19]

While Moses portrayed God as basically a transactional being – blessings for obeying all commands vs. punishment for disobedience – Jesus' image of his Father was one of extreme generosity to all! He even referred to Yahweh as *Abba*, an Aramaic word that means "daddy" or "papa."

If Jesus embodied the image of the transactional God that so many well-meaning people of faith hold today, here is what he could have done differently:

- He could have put leprosy on those who were not meeting biblical standards.
- He could have waved his hand, and the religious outcasts would have dropped dead due to their wicked and immoral behavior. Instead, he had parties with them in their own homes!

---

[17] Matthew 6:25-30
[18] John 9:2
[19] Luke 13:5

- He could have called fire down from heaven on a town who wouldn't accept him, as his disciples begged him to do. Instead, he corrected his followers' perception of God.[20]
- At his crucifixion, he could have authorized thousands of angels to set him free and destroy the earth.[21]

What people often miss in these passages is that Jesus, even though quoted as saying he came to fulfill and not abolish the laws of Moses, in effect still contradicted Moses' teachings and laws! Many may be uncomfortable with my statement, but the bottom line is that Jesus's understanding of the Father was very different to that of Moses. Jesus's understanding was relational – based on his own spiritual experiences with his heavenly Father.

I have come to see that when one personally experiences the profound love that God has for each one of us, one can no longer weaponize Bible verses against those whom God loves and accepts.

It is not enough to conform ourselves to the Bible! Sadly, it seems that those who insist on conforming to scripture tend to conform to the Old Testament images of God's judgment, anger, and extreme punishment for disobedience. *It is choosing an image of a transactional God over a relational one.* Instead, we must inform our understanding of

---

[20] Luke 9:54
[21] Matthew 26:23

34

God through our own personal experiences of him that track with how Jesus described him.

When one senses kindness, acceptance, and love toward other individuals – whether of a different race, nationality, political belief, or sexual orientation – one is actually sensing the love of God flow through him or her as it did with Jesus. Look at these beautiful verses from 1st John. Notice how relational the description of love is between God and us, and us toward others. It even goes as far as using the Greek word *ginosko* when it describes "knowing" God, which was a term that could also refer to sexual intimacy. This passage does not focus on an intellectual understanding of God, but rather an experiential relationship that one can have with the Divine.

> *Dear friends, let us continue to love one another, for **love comes from God. Anyone who loves is a child of God and knows God. But anyone who does not love does not know God, for God is love.** God showed how much he loved us by sending his one and only Son into the world so that we might have eternal life through him. This is real love—not that we loved God, but that he loved us and sent his Son as a sacrifice to take away our sins. Dear friends, since God loved us that much,*

we surely ought to love each other. ***No one has ever seen God. But if we love each other, God lives in us, and his love is brought to full expression in us.***[22] [Emphasis mine]

Every one of us, no matter who we are or how we are defined by others, are deeply and passionately loved by our heavenly Abba!

How we understand God is extremely important, especially with the sensitive subject this book addresses.

---

[22] 1 John 4:7-12

CHAPTER 4 – The "Not-So-Cool Kids" at the Party!

As I noted earlier, I was raised in typical fundamental/evangelical churches in which my father was the pastor. When I was in high school in the late 1960s–early 1970s, the Jesus Movement was in full swing, where thousands of hippies and others in the counterculture of the day had encounters with Christ that changed their lives. The biggest "moral" concerns that many churches had about such people were the long hair and beards on the men, and the introduction of Christian rock music (country music today has more rock 'n roll than those songs did) with the added shock of using guitars and drums in church! Everyone knew that the musical instruments approved by God were pianos and Hammond B-3 organs (perhaps sent down by God when He delivered the first full copy of the King James Bible straight from heaven)!

Ah, simpler times...

Though I was a "preacher's kid" and not a hippie, the Jesus Movement had a powerful impact on my life that continues to this day. Some of my closest friends had life-changing encounters with Christ during that era. It was like a bright, shining light during the dark times of assassinations, the Vietnam War, and race riots.

Fast-forward several decades.

In 2023 the movie *Jesus Revolution* was released. It was a retelling of the Jesus Movement that had impacted so many millions, including myself. The actor Kelsey Grammar brilliantly portrayed Pastor Chuck Smith, a conservative pastor who came to embrace this "revolution" that ultimately transformed his little church into the great Calvary Chapel Movement. Early in the movie we watched how some members of his little congregation strongly resisted the long-haired, bearded, bare-footed youth who started attending his church, bringing their clothing styles and "hippie" music with them.

As my wife and I sat in the theater one afternoon watching the movie, I started wondering who were the "hippies" of our current generation: those considered outcasts, disgusting, and unwanted in so many churches?

As sociologists will tell us, humans are naturally wired to form "ingroups vs. outgroups." We all want to feel superior to someone else. That's human nature, and it manifests in many ways:

- Economics. Wealthy vs. poor. White collar vs. blue collar.
- Politics. Democrats vs. Republicans
- Education. College-educated or PhDs vs. high school or GED graduates
- Racial. In addition to overt racism with which most are familiar, there are subtle forms that many who would not consider themselves

racist still participate in – such as ethnic jokes. Having lived in several parts of the United States I have noticed the same jokes are used for different nationalities who are considered inferior: Polish, Finnish, Jewish, African American, and Mexican, to name a few. Some in the south tell jokes about "Yankees" while people in the north mock "rednecks" from the south. In England the Irish can be the butt of jokes. Canadians joke about "Newfies" – people from Newfoundland. These types of attitudes are a worldwide phenomenon because it is in our nature to want to feel superior to somebody.

- Gender. Who hasn't laughed at "Blonde" jokes, where the joke is almost always about a dumb blonde female? One ancient Jewish prayer by a rabbi included thanks to God for not making him a woman!

- Religion. This seems almost too obvious to mention as there are many possible applications, but I want to focus on one particular attitude. In one of Jesus' stories, he compared the prayer of a Pharisee (who would have been considered devout, pious, and strict in his religion) with that of a loathed tax collector who worked for the despised Romans and was considered scum of the earth by that society:

"... The Pharisee stood by himself and prayed this prayer: 'I thank you, God, that I am not a sinner like everyone else. For I don't cheat, I don't sin, and I don't commit adultery. I'm certainly not like that tax collector! I fast twice a week, and I give you a tenth of my income.' But the tax collector stood at a distance and dared not even lift his eyes to heaven as he prayed. Instead, he beat his chest in sorrow, saying, 'O God, be merciful to me, for I am a sinner.' I tell you, this sinner, not the Pharisee, returned home justified before God. For those who exalt themselves will be humbled, and those who humble themselves will be exalted."[23]

This is a cautionary tale for all of us. It is easy to compare ourselves with someone who we perceive to be inferior to us morally, but the attitude of the heart is what God gazes at.

It is noteworthy that Jesus tended to side with the outsiders or outgroups – those in society the religious crowd rejected. Think of the groups with whom he partied:

---

[23] Luke 18:12-24

- Tax collectors and sinners (those who ignored the rules and practices of the religiously fastidious)[24]
- Women: allowing them to be part of his entourage; consenting to let a woman touch him by pouring expensive perfume on him and washing his feet with her tears – a sensual act even in our time but very scandalous back then;[25] talking to a woman alone without a male chaperone, as was the custom in his day (and as it still is in some Muslim societies)[26]
- Samaritans: considered 'half-breeds' by the dominant culture in Israel and who were religious opponents with their own temple, rituals, and clergy. Jesus spent time teaching in Sychar, one of their cities. The hero of his most famous story was a Samaritan, not the "righteous" religious leaders. Jesus's personal conversation with the woman at the well outside Sychar is not only notable because she was an unaccompanied woman but that she was also Samaritan.[27]
- Gentiles (non-Jews). considered unclean based both on their race and their foreign customs. Jesus interacted with them: healing

---

[24] Matthew 9:10-11; 11:19; Mark 2:15-17; Luke 7:34; 15:1
[25] Luke 7:36-38
[26] John 4
[27] Ibid.

41

the servant of a Roman officer,[28] exorcising a demon from the daughter of a Syrophoenician woman,[29] feeding 4000 gentiles in northern Galilee,[30] talking to Greek individuals who sought him out.[31]

So, acknowledging that humans tend to form in-groups and out-groups is easy to do. What is more challenging is when leaders - both cultural and religious – are determined to enforce those group boundaries.

Which brings us to our next chapter...

---

[28] Matthew 8:13
[29] Mark 7:24-30
[30] Mark 7: 31; 8: 1-9
[31] John 12:22

CHAPTER 5 – "This Party Needs Security!"

The Gatekeepers

As I pointed out in the last chapter, religious movements tend to specialize in deciding who is "in" and who is "out." It is an impulse that is hard to resist, especially if the members are convinced that what they believe is "what the Bible says."

Ironically, this demonstrates overconfidence since there are thousands of denominations and independent groups who also claim they believe only what the Bible says but disagree with each other (but I digress). Humility is sadly not a major characteristic of so many of us. Hubris strikes again!

Of course, in-groups vs. out-groups are not new. It extends back to ancient biblical practices from Moses' law and was enforced at times during Israel's history. For example:

> [King Jehoida] *also stationed gatekeepers at the gates of the LORD's Temple to keep out those who for any reason were ceremonially unclean.*[32]

Imagine – trying to keep people out of church!

---

[32] 2 Chronicles 23:19

Here is a partial list of people who were not welcome to join a worship service as they were considered "unclean" (from the Book of Leviticus unless otherwise noted):

PEOPLE WHO WEREN'T WELCOME IN "CHURCH" (COULDN'T ENTER THE TEMPLE)

1. A woman after giving birth (12:55). The mother was considered unclean for 41 days if the baby was a boy, 80 days if it was a girl!
2. Skin diseases or injuries that haven't healed (leprosy, boils, burns) (chapter 13)
3. People with bodily discharges (blood, semen, menstrual flow, etc.) (chapter 15)
4. Gentiles (non-Israelites)
5. People who have touched a dead body or animal carcass (21:1-4; Numbers 19:11)
6. Men with emasculated or mutilated genitals (Deuteronomy 23:1)
7. People who were born illegitimately *plus* their descendants for 10 generations! Think about this: if your great, great, great, great, great, great, great, grandfather was illegitimate, you couldn't go to church! (Deuteronomy 23:2)

8.   More stringent laws for priests: no one blind, hunchbacked, or lame could be accepted; priests could have no birth defect, broken foot or hand, or eczema; also, priests who were dwarves or eunuchs (lack of male testicles) could not serve (21:1-21).

Some of the above prohibitions would last a short time. Minor infractions allowed a person to be considered unclean only until nightfall, others perhaps up to one week. A casual look at the list, however, demonstrates that some of those restrictions were either long-lasting or permanent.

One could point out that some of the above restrictions were practical. Following them would reduce the spread of infectious diseases, especially in an ancient society without the benefits of modern medicine and proper hygiene. And that's a good point. However, some of the prohibitions would not fall in that category.

And throughout these passages one often reads the phrase, "the LORD said to Moses." So according to the text it was Yahweh who made the laws; Moses was simply the "court reporter" writing down what he heard.

Cleanliness practices continued during the Second Temple period (the time of Jesus). There were ritual baths that one must take before entering the temple area to be "clean." Once on the temple grounds, there were outer courts where gentiles had to remain; special areas for women who were not ritually impure (see the above list). Only Jewish men who were not unclean (again see the list) were allowed to go into the temple area proper.

However, Jesus had a different idea!

He taught that it was what comes out of the heart—hatred, lust, lying, pride, etc.—that defiles a person, not the strict purification laws that religious folk held so highly.[33] Many of the people Jesus healed were ceremonially unclean. When he touched them or was touched by them, he technically also became ceremonially unclean!

Yet that did not stop him from touching and healing them.

As we saw in the last chapter, Jesus, who Christians believe led a sinless life, was welcomed and loved by those who were considered outcasts by the religious authorities. As the Gospel of Mark says, "The common people received him gladly."[34]

Many committed Christians have few good friends who are not also believers. There are several reasons for this. Some spend so much time and energy in church or doing religious activities that it is a challenge to spend quality time even with their own family, much less their neighbors. Others are more comfortable hanging out with their fellow church members than with people who may not share their values. Some feel that if they must spend

---

[33] Matthew 15:10-20
[34] Mark 12:37 (KJV)

time with "normal" people they have to always be watching for an opportunity to proselytize. And sadly, some are afraid to hang out with "sinners," however defined, lest they become contaminated and become "sinners" themselves.

My observation has been that normal, everyday people who are not deeply religious seldom feel comfortable hanging out with devout, pious people.

And yet, Jesus was invited by such people (or invited himself on occasion) to have meals and hang out with them. With Jesus the out-group became the in-group, as he demonstrated in his teachings and stories.[35] Some have called it the "great reversal."

Fear of the "Other"

As humans, it is hard not to categorize people into in-or-out groups based on race, economics, nationality, sexuality, or other factors. Sometimes one of the roots of prejudice is fear of others who are different, especially if we don't know anyone from the other group or have had a negative experience with such an individual.

I saw this when I was 11 years old, and it left a lasting impression on me. In the 1960s my father pastored a conservative white congregation in the

---

[35] Check out the following: Matthew 8:11-12; 9:12-13; 20:16; Mark 10:31; Luke 13:28-30

Midwest. One Sunday morning a young Caucasian woman walked into our church at the beginning of the service. She did not know anyone there and no one knew how or why she decided to visit. In her arms was an extremely cute little baby who was obviously biracial (half Caucasian/ half African American). She found a pew in which to sit and remained through the service. The baby slept the whole time and created no disturbance. After the sermon and closing hymn, she slipped out quietly with her baby. I recall only one or two people shaking her hand, but no one showed much interest in her or the baby.

What I will never forget was one of the elders approached my father after the service and suggested they should ask her not to attend the church again since her baby was mixed race. My father, to his credit, stood firm against any such action and addressed the attitudes behind it.

Of course, it was all moot anyway, since the woman never came back. I have often wondered if she sensed the attitudes of at least some of the attendees that morning. Coming for encouragement or help, she was met with rejection and judgment.

What is also heartbreaking is that this congregation was made up of decent, hard-working, moral blue-collar workers. They were not members of the Klu Klux Klan. They would not have joined radical white supremacist movements or waved confederate flags. Yet a little biracial baby and its mother were still not welcome.

Substitute the issue of race with economics or human sexuality and this scene plays out in churches across the nation every Sunday. Perhaps it is time to pull out those rubber bracelets from a couple decades ago, stare at them for a few minutes, and ask ourselves, "What would Jesus do?"

Many of us need a new job description.

Instead of seeing ourselves as God's appointed gate keepers, we need to become gate openers!

It is time for us to stop worrying about guarding the fort and instead welcome all whom God loves - even if they are different from us.

A BRIEF INTERLUDE

So far, we have seen that God's kingdom is described as a giant, wonderful, blow-out party. This scriptural metaphor demonstrates how generous, kind, and welcoming our heavenly Father is, and how deep his love encompasses everyone and everything.

We will continue to see that the Bible, at its very best, helps us know and understand Jesus, and consequently know what our heavenly Father is like, since when we see (and understand) Jesus, we can then see (and understand) the Father.

However, that same Bible that has enlightened and comforted billions of people over the centuries can be weaponized to cause great damage and destruction...

Wounding

Condemnation.

.   Exclusion.

As we pivot to the next section of this book, you are about to read a dramatic story of how scriptures were weaponized in a way that almost cost a woman her life. We will then examine in detail how certain Bible verses have been weaponized against the LGBTQ+ community to hurt, condemn, and exclude them from God's generous celebration.

Finally, we will explore ways to align with God's heart and mind, as seen through Jesus.

Let's move on to the next exciting part...

CHAPTER 6 – "I Guess *She's* Not Invited!"

It was *not* supposed to end like this.

One minute she and Levi were in the throes of passion in her bed. The next thing she knew, a group of angry men broke down the bedroom door, grabbed her by her hair and arms, and yelled insults at her as they began to roughly drag her out of her house. As they reached the front door, one of the men yelled, "Stop just a moment!" He marched back into the bedroom. She hoped he was bringing Levi. Maybe Levi could talk the men down out of their frenzy or at least protect her from the worst of the violence.

But Levi was nowhere to be found.

Instead, the man returned from the bedroom with a small blanket. Not much, but it would at least cover part of her naked body. Since the blanket was not adequate to cover her completely, the woman adjusted it to cover her back and head so at least the gawking passers-by might not recognize her. She bent over to hide her body as much as she could as she was simultaneously pushed and dragged through the city streets.

It wasn't supposed to end like this.

How could something so beautiful, so exciting, so longed for since she was of marrying age, turn into this horrid, humiliating, heartbreak for the last hour of her wretched life?

53

Well, she reminded herself, her whole life had not been wretched. Leah (for that was her name) had a normal childhood in her village in the Galilee region, playing with other children her age when she was small. As the children approached adolescence, the boys were not allowed to hang out with the girls. Besides, the boys spent part of their days in school if they were lucky enough to attend or spent time learning the trades of the fathers. Each girl was taught how to cook, sew, clean, care for babies and small children, with the hopes that her father would find a suitable husband for her.

Leah had already picked who *she* wanted to marry. Levi was a handsome young man with kind eyes coupled with a mischievous smile. Even though they were not allowed to interact with each other socially as they got older, Leah fantasized about marrying Levi, having children together, growing old together. When she saw him on the main street of their town, her heart would flutter, and she would blush. She could only hope that he felt the same thing.

It was not to be.

When she was fourteen, Leah's father arranged for her marriage to a young man from a neighboring town. Avram, her new husband, was six years older than Leah, and had already begun to show a real aptitude for business. He never treated her badly, and as he became more prosperous, he provided her with a nicer home and finer clothes. Eventually they

54

were wealthy enough to hire servants to handle the cooking and cleaning. But his first love was his business, not his wife. They didn't fight and seldom argued. But there was no passion, and only a superficial warmth toward each other.

Within two years, Avram realized he could make much more money if they moved to Jerusalem, the capital city of Judea, than if he stayed in Galilee. Leah was not happy leaving the small town and the people she had known her whole life but had no choice but to follow her husband. Occasionally, her mind would wander, and she would think about Levi, wondering what he was doing. Was he married? Did he have children? Was he happy? She would never know.

Until...

One day in Jerusalem Avram rushed home early from work and exclaimed, "Leah, have the servants prepare a feast. I ran into a stranger at the market who is here from Galilee for the annual Tabernacle festival. While we were talking, I learned that he was looking for a place to stay, so I invited him to dinner. We can put him up in our guest room. Leah sighed. It was not unusual for Avram to bring someone home for a meal. He was always networking. Leah hurriedly planned the menu with her servants and confirmed that the guest room was prepared.

Two hours later there was a knock at the door. Avram, excited to see his guest, answered the door himself and invited the guest inside. He called for Leah to come meet his visitor. As she came around the corner to the entryway, she was momentarily stunned but immediately tried to disguise her shock. Standing before her was Levi! He was obviously older than when she last saw him several years before. He was not the skinny teen she remembered. She noticed he had filled out nicely; a little more muscular, a trimmed beard, and still had that mischievous smile. But would he even remember her?

Avram stretched out his arm toward his wife and announced, "May I present my lovely wife Leah!"

Levi looked Leah in the eye, smiled and said, "It is an honor to meet the wife of my new friend." Leah stared back at him and replied, "The honor is mine, sir." At that moment Leah knew two things – Levi recognized her, and she wanted him! She turned and went to the kitchen, while Avram and Levi reclined at the table to eat. The servants brought in roasted lamb, fresh bread, and pomegranates. The two men shared their stories with each other. Leah, eavesdropped from the kitchen, learning that Levi had married; he and his wife had three children, and he had come to Jerusalem with some friends for the festival, leaving his wife and children home in Galilee. Avram's conversation largely focused on his business transactions, the economy of Jerusalem, and the financial benefits he gained from the annual feasts.

Finally, after a full meal and copious amounts of wine, they all retired to their separate rooms for the night.

The next morning, Avram was up early and out the door. There was money to be made with all the thousands of people here in Jerusalem for the feast, and he wanted his share!

Leah had risen soon after and was sitting at the dining table, thinking about last night's events, when Levi came down from his room. He placed a hand on her shoulder as he walked by. In that time, touching a woman to whom one was not married was forbidden. Leah didn't flinch when he touched her. For some reason it seemed so natural. When he returned, he asked if he could sit down with her for a few minutes.

Also forbidden.

Her heart began to race but she nodded.

When they began to talk, it seemed like a torrent of pent-up feelings hidden behind a dam overflowed for each of them. While they both knew what they were doing was wrong, it was as if they couldn't help themselves. With Avram off at work, the servants away for the morning, and Levi having nowhere he had to be, they both stood. Leah took Levi's hand, gently led him to her bedroom, and closed the door.

What they had not considered were the neighbors, a few who had seen Levi arrive at the house the previous night. It was also noted that Avram had left early in the morning without his new friend. The friend and Leah were still in the house. At the very least this was inappropriate. At worst it was criminal.

Leah and Levi also had not considered that some of the neighbors in this wealthier neighborhood were lawyers and strict religious leaders called Pharisees. This quickly became more complicated, as some of the men simply wanted to accost the two lovers (if that was what was going on), drag them out of the city, and stone them to death as prescribed by the law of Moses. Others had a different agenda. A Teacher from the Galilee region had come to Jerusalem for the feast and was instilling ideas of which these leaders did not approve. They had attempted on different occasions to confront the Teacher and make a fool of him, but he always turned the tables on them in front of the people, making the leaders look like idiots.

But now here was a solution to their dilemma. They could use this couple to trap the Teacher into saying something against Moses's law, and then they could prosecute and get rid of him.

But where was the Teacher? He had left the city the night before and they weren't sure where he was. About that time, one of the servants spoke up: "I saw the teacher in the outer courts of the temple mid-morning. He was sitting with about fifty or sixty people around him and he was teaching them."

That settled it for the group of men, which had now grown almost to the size of a mob. They would arrest the couple, take them to the Teacher, and after they trapped him, they would take the couple out of the city and stone them.

Being roughly dragged and pushed through the streets, Leah was not sure where they were headed, though she suspected that wherever that was, it would not go well for her. As they came closer to the huge temple built by King Herod years ago, Leah became confused. Why were they bringing a half-naked woman onto temple property? This was going to be worse than she could imagine.

Suddenly and without notice, they shoved her to the ground. All became quiet.

Without looking up, she peered through the blanket partially covering her head at her surroundings. It seemed surreal. To her left, a crowd of people sat close together. They were staring at her in shock. The men who had grabbed her stood between her and the crowd, facing her. To her right sat a solitary man. He stood and gazed at the mob of men. "What do you want?" he asked.

The leader of the mob spoke first. "Teacher, we caught this woman in the *very act* of adultery." "Now," the man said with mock sincerity, "the law of Moses says she should be stoned to death. What say you?"

Leah slowly turned her head slightly to see who was speaking, and as she did, she saw something that shocked her more than all the events of this morning put together. Levi was standing with the men who had dragged her through the streets, a large stone in his hand. She immediately realized what had happened. When the men barged into her bedroom, they had gone for her first. Levi jumped out of bed, scooped up his clothes, and exited through a side door of her room. Since they were distracted by the naked woman and would not recognize him since he was from Galilee, he hid behind a neighboring building while he dressed, smoothed his hair, grabbed a softball-sized stone, and joined the mob as they proceeded toward the temple, no one the wiser. And in that instant, she realized his motive: dead people don't talk! Killing her would solve his immediate problem of facing his wife and Leah's husband.

Leah also noticed that Levi's face seemed to reflect hardness, but there was fear in his eyes. She had been betrayed by the one she had fantasized about from afar, betrayed by the only man she had ever loved.

Yes, this day was getting worse, if that was even possible!

Her thoughts were brought back to the men who hauled her there. They were taunting the Teacher. She glanced to her right. The Teacher had crouched down and was using the index finger of his right hand to write in the dirt. He seemed to be thinking… or praying.

"What, no clever one-liners?"

"No snappy comeback?"

"Quit procrastinating! What do you think we should do?"

After a moment everything went still. The Teacher stood and looked at the men with anger in his eyes. Leah couldn't help but look up at him, and when she saw his expression, she first thought it was towards her. But he wasn't looking at her. He was looking at the men.

The Teacher spoke one sentence that would reverberate through the ages.

"Whoever is without sin can throw the first stone."

There was a roaring silence. The Teacher dropped back into a crouching position and started writing in the dirt again.

Finally, two of the older men dropped their stones on the ground with a thump, turned around and slowly disappeared into the crowded temple. Leah was too afraid to watch, but she could hear thump...thump...thump of stones as they hit the ground. The younger men, who had been the most intense and roughest in their treatment of Leah, dropped their heads and their rocks last, and left as well. It seemed the Teacher had taken the wind out of their sails. Even Levi, with a look of embarrassment as he glanced at Leah, gave a subtle nod, turned, and walked away.

With the mob fully dissipated, the Teacher took Leah's chin in his hand and gently said, "Look at me." As she did, she noticed the glare of anger that was in the Teacher's eyes as he looked at the men was now replaced with something that was almost indescribable. It was love, but not a lustful, manipulating, manufactured love. No, it was a deep sense of pure, genuine, kindness... compassion... forgiveness.

The Teacher then smiled and as he waved his hand in front of him said, "Look around. Where are the men who accused you?"

Leah looked in shock as she saw the only ones there were the crowd who had been listening to the Teacher before this episode all began. She replied with shock and amazement, "There's no one there. They have all left!"

The Teacher, with that compassionate look still on his face, softly said, "I don't condemn you, either." He asked Leah what her name was, and when she told him, he smiled again and then asked the women who had been listening to his teaching if they had any extra garments they could give Leah. Several responded, and soon, though not all the colors matched, she had at least retrieved her modesty for her walk home.

Before she left, she kneeled in front of the Teacher, gratefully weeping. She thanked him for saving her life, forgiving her, and showing her kindness. Once more, he lifted her up, this time to her feet. He smiled again and whispered, not as a command with an implied threat but rather a gentle admonition, "And Leah, don't do this again."

CHAPTER 7 – Misreading the Party Invitation

Hold on to the dramatic story of Leah in the last chapter. We'll come back to it in a moment. But first, a quick vignette...

A young couple are approaching their second wedding anniversary. The husband, though still rather new at this, knows anniversaries are important – especially to his wife. A week before the anniversary arrives, they have this conversation:

Him: *Hey, honey, what would you like for our anniversary next week?*

Her: *Ohhh, nothing...*

Him: *Are you sure? I'll be happy to get something for you.*

Her: *Yeah, nothing...*

Him (thinking): *Whew! What a relief! I thought I would have to go shopping, find something she would like, buy it, wrap it up or put it in a gift bag with that weird colored tissue paper. I think I just dodged a bullet!*

Her (thinking): *I hope he loves me and knows me well enough that he will get me a thoughtful, beautiful, and expensive present.*

It doesn't take a genius to figure out that both are headed for a crushing disappointment. I know this from personal, uh, observation of, uh... others.

It is easy to see why it failed. The young husband took his wife's words *literally* but missed what she was *really* saying. He thought he knew what she really wanted but didn't.

Adventure in Missing the Point

Sadly, many times Bible readers make the same mistake the young man made with his wife. We take verses literally, but we miss the underlying message. We forget the awesome heart and mind of our Heavenly Father, who invites everyone to his party!

When this happens, certain Bible verses become stones in the hands of people that, in the name of holiness or fidelity to scripture (at least as they understand it), can be thrown to hurt, drive away, and deeply harm those who are created and loved by God.

Oddly, when I discuss with others the implications of the story of Leah in chapter six, their main "take-away" often is that Jesus told her not to sin again.

What?!

Really?!

It is almost always interpreted as Jesus issuing a divine threat, "You got away with it this time, but next time you won't be so lucky!"

"A part of human nature is to gather stones to throw rather than garments to cover."

The deeper problem is that a part of human nature is to gather stones to throw rather than garments to cover; to deflect or project our prejudices and judgments onto others instead of a much-needed introspection. In modern times, scripture has been used against various people groups: women, slaves, divorcees, hippies, and now the gay community.

To use a metaphor from the Old Testament, we have stony hearts – hearts of stone – rather than hearts of flesh. And out of the abundance of our hearts come pride, anger, rage, and judgment. People with soft hearts do not throw hard stones! Using proof texts from scripture does not alter the fact that many of us have cold, rigid hearts.

In the following chapters we are going to examine four "stones" used from the Bible to misread the party's invitation, thus excluding and condemning members of the gay community.

CHAPTER 8 – The Stone of Sodom

One of the passages in the Bible that is used to bash homosexuals is the ancient story of the "Five Cities of the Plain" – more popularly known as the story of Sodom and Gomorrah.

Here is the "Sunday School" version – you know, the somewhat age-appropriate spin used to tell the story to children: the Bible hero Abraham had a nephew named Lot who lived in a very bad city with lots of bad people. God decided to destroy the city and sent two angels to get Lot and his family out first. Some bad people came to Lot's house to hurt him and the angels, but the angels protected him and got Lot and his family out of the city just as fire started falling from heaven. The angels told Lot and his family to keep running and to not even turn around and look at the fire. Lot's wife turned around to look at the fire and became a statue of salt.

End of story.

Except it's not the end or even the beginning.

Before we discuss why this story is used as a punching bag against gays and others, we need to understand the background a little more, for this story didn't just happen in a vacuum. And the account is fascinating.

Abraham and his nephew Lot lived in what is now Israel. They were both extremely wealthy (remember this was an agricultural-based society). They would be more like very wealthy ranchers –

owning huge herds of cattle and flocks of sheep and goats and having many servants to run the businesses.

Because large operations such as theirs needed a tremendous amount of land for grazing as well as good water sources, conflicts arose between their herdsmen (this has all the makings of a great western if it was set in Wyoming in the late 1800s). Since Abraham owned so much land, he wanted to keep peace with Lot, so he suggested they split up into different directions. Abraham, being the good uncle he was, gave Lot the first choice of where to go.

At this point a picture begins to emerge about Lot's character and it is not very attractive. Though Abraham had taken his nephew under his wing from the time they moved from what is modern-day Syria, Lot appears to be more self-centered than his loving uncle. Since he was given first pick of land, he selfishly chose the best land for himself – green, grassy fields with an abundance of water. It was also close to five cities – including Sodom and Gomorrah. He eventually settled in the city of Sodom.

We do not know if he sold his business and lived in luxury in the city or turned the management of his farming business over to others. We do know that he eventually married (perhaps a woman from the community) and they had two daughters who themselves were eventually engaged to local guys. In one New Testament passage, he was called "righteous Lot" who was troubled by the violent and greedy culture of Sodom – but not troubled enough to leave.[36]

The cities at that time were like miniature city states, each ruled by their own king. A little later, four kings from the north attacked the five cities, captured the local kings and took all their belongings as spoils of war. They also kidnapped Lot. When Abraham heard about Lot's predicament, Abraham took 300 of his servants (definitely a very wealthy man), fought and defeated the aggressors, and rescued not only Lot and the five kings, but also recovered all that was taken from them. Abraham refused to receive any rewards for his courageous efforts. His reason: he did not want to be beholden to them so they could brag about how they made him rich (which of course he already was). He seemed to know the character of the kings and their subjects and did not trust them.

More about Lot in a few moments...

Later back home, Abraham was outside his tent and saw three "men" walking past. According to the Bible, he somehow intuited that the "men" were actually Yahweh and two angels, all in human form.[37] He convinced them to stop and have a meal with him. He washed their feet, not only as a good host of that era but also to show subservience. He then served a veal meal with fresh bread. After

---

[36] 2 Peter 2:7
[37] You can read the whole story in Genesis 18-19

lunch, Yahweh told Abraham that they are going to destroy Sodom and Gomorrah because of their great wickedness. Abraham was alarmed. He had recently rescued his nephew only to be told that his nephew would be among the victims of the coming judgment.

So, Abraham began to negotiate with God, asking if God would destroy the city if there were 50 "righteous" people in it. Now we moderns usually associate the term "righteous" with pious, church-going people who behave themselves. However, the Hebrew word implies being just – helping people who have been treated unjustly, especially those who are oppressed and downtrodden by society.[38] God agreed not to destroy the city if there were 50 "just" people.

Abraham thought about it for a moment and realized finding 50 "just" people in that city might be a stretch. (It was indeed a nasty place.)

So Abraham bargained God down to 40.

Then 30.

Then 20.

Then 10.

Think about it – in a city of perhaps 1000 people (we don't know how big it was, but this number will work to make my point), Abraham wasn't sure that even 10 people could be found who acted justly toward others!

---

[38] The Hebrew word is *tsaddiyq* (pronounced tsad-**deek**), often used to describe justice or someone who practices justice.

Yahweh disappeared, and the two angels (who still looked like men) proceeded on their journey to Sodom. The angels found Lot sitting at the city gates.[39] In that era, city gates would be the equivalent of our county courthouse or city hall where the city leaders decided on legal issues and set policy. Lot had evidently risen to a level of leadership, meaning he was well-known and was part of the city elite.

Lot invited the angels to his home for a feast. While they were eating, some men of the city started pounding on Lot's door, demanding that he send the two "men" out so they could gang-rape them. Lot went out, shut the door behind them, and being the "good" father he was, offered up both his daughters to be gang-raped instead. This incensed the crowd even more, and the angels had to grab Lot by the collar and pull him inside for safety. The next morning, the angels told Lot to urgently get his family – his wife, daughters, and their fiancés – to hurry up and get out, because the city was about to be destroyed. His daughters' fiancés thought they were joking.[40]

Still Lot *hesitated* about leaving.

The angels finally grabbed his hand and those of his wife and daughters and dragged them out of the city (the girls' fiancés' did not join them.) The angels told Lot and his family to run as fast as they could

---

[39] Genesis 19:1
[40] Verse 14

to the mountains, but Lot pleaded with them to allow his family to go to a little village instead that was a day away. The angels agreed, and the family hurriedly made their way to the village.

That night, the Bible says that fire and brimstone fell from heaven and destroyed Sodom, Gomorrah, and the neighboring towns and villages. Though told not to, Lot's wife looked back toward Sodom. In Sunday School, we were told that she glanced back and – presto – she became a pillar of salt. However, the text says that she was "behind" Lot, so we don't know if she was a few feet away or much more. The original language indicates that it wasn't just a glance (such as out of curiosity) but rather that she gazed or stood there contemplating, maybe feeling regret for all the people she was leaving or the loss of her possessions. Since they left Sodom in the morning and the fireworks didn't begin until nightfall, she may have decided this was a fool's errand to go running to the mountains and perhaps turned around and started back home. This is implied in one of Jesus' teachings that we will see below.

We will never know exactly what she was thinking, but it didn't turn out well for her.

It is also telling that the Bible says that God saved Lot and his family, not because they were necessarily just, but as a favor to Abraham![41]

---

[41] Verse 29

But the story isn't over.

Lot and his two daughters left the little village in which he had begged the angels to let him stay, and went to the mountains after all, hiding in a cave. The girls realized that being cave dwellers, there were not many options to marry and have children, which would be considered a humiliating disgrace in their culture.

They hatched a plan.

The older daughter got her father very, very drunk, and once that happened, she had sex with him and was impregnated.

The younger daughter followed her older sister's example the next night with comparable results.

The two babies born to them were named Moab and Ammon, whose descendants centuries later expanded into two large tribes that were mortal enemies of Israel.[42]

So, the ignominious story of Lot ends with double incest and the beginning of future adversaries of God's people.

Many centuries later Israel's prophets railed against Israel and Judah (the descendants of Abraham now divided into two countries – long story) for their oppressive attitudes and actions toward the poor and defenseless, comparing them to Sodom.

---

[42] Genesis 19:37-38

The ancient prophet Ezekiel, speaking in the name of Yahweh, explained why Yahweh destroyed Sodom:

Sodom's sins were pride, gluttony, and laziness, while the poor and needy suffered outside her door. She was proud and committed detestable sins, so I wiped her out, as you have seen.[43]

Even Jesus, when talking about the coming destruction of Jerusalem and the temple, likened his generation to Sodom, and used Lot's wife as a cautionary tale:

*"And the world will be as it was in the days of Lot. People went about their daily business—eating and drinking, buying and selling, farming and building—until the morning Lot left Sodom. Then fire and burning sulfur rained down from heaven and destroyed them all. Yes, it will be 'business as usual' right up to the day when the Son of Man is revealed. On that day a person out on the deck of a roof must not go down into the house to pack. **A person out in the field must not return home. Remember what happened to***

---

[43] Ezekiel 16:49-50

Lot's wife! [Emphasis mine.] *If you cling to your life, you will lose it, and if you let your life go, you will save it."*[44]

The way Jesus described it, it all sounded normal enough at Sodom, except for the earlier writings that described horrendous deeds done there. As noted above, he also implied that Lot's wife didn't just glance back but may have headed home.

What's the Point?

To many of my readers, this whole story seems incredulous. Some would say that it was constructed generations later to explain some natural phenomena such as a volcano or meteor shower. Scientists and archaeologists have noted that, around this time, there is evidence of a strong earthquake that released gases and oil that had been underground which exploded, causing massive destruction. Here is a report from Biblical Archaeology Review:

> *Across Tall el-Hammam* [ruins from an ancient city in the area], *archaeologists found widespread evidence of an intense conflagration that left the Middle Bronze Age city in ruins. They found scorched*

---

[44] Luke 17: 28-33

foundations and floors buried under nearly 3 feet of dark grey ash, as well as dozens of pottery sherds covered with a frothy, "melted" surface; the glassy appearance indicates that they were briefly exposed to temperatures well in excess of 2,000 degrees Fahrenheit, the approximate heat of volcanic magma. Such evidence suggests the city and its environs were catastrophically destroyed in a sudden and extreme conflagration.[45]

Evidently something happened in that area that somewhat corroborates the biblical narrative. My point, however, is not to defend the story as actual history or to raise doubts about it. Rather, this story has been used as a bludgeon against gays because of the gang rape scene in Sodom, implying that God destroyed the cities over homosexual activity.[46]

This is the 3000-pound elephant in the room. So, let's address it.

---

[45] Collins, Steven. "Where is Sodom? The Case for Tall el-Hammam." *Biblical archaeology review* 39, no. 2 (2013).

[46] It is worth noting that, historically, a common phrase used in our culture for homosexual activity is "sodomy" which comes directly from the Sodom story in the Bible.

Gang Rape

This point has often been missed when using the text against the LGBTQ+ community. I think all would agree that gang rape is a horrendous action perpetrated against another human created in God's image. It is not primarily about having sex; rather it is about violence and domination over the victim. Its victims very often feel intense shame and sometimes self-blame, while the victimizers mock the weaknesses and the inferiority of the victim. Sex is simply the conduit used to commit the act of violence.

Think of it this way: if the crowd of men had been satisfied with gang-raping Lot's two daughters (as he offered to let them do), would that have been better?

Of course not!

This vicious, sadistic act was not about sex—gay or straight—but hardcore violence. The gang hated and resented Lot, accusing him of being an outsider who moved to Sodom, rose through the ranks, and now sat in a leadership position judging them.[47] This indicates they were motivated by envy, malice, and racial bigotry.

And that is what the God who is love detests.

So, what is the point of the "Sodom" story?

---

[47] Genesis 19:19

Remember, according to the biblical story, God had already decided to destroy the city *before* the gang rape episode (though perhaps this wasn't the only time that had happened.) The sins that brought destruction were the ones that Christians seldom hear about from their pastors – gluttony, pride, laziness, and especially being insensitive to the needs of the poor. Sadly, to use Jesus' analogy, it is easier to go after the splinter in another's eye than to deal with the log in ours.

It seems to me, then, that to use this story as a battering ram against the LGBTQ+ community is an adventure in missing the point.

CHAPTER 9 – The Stone of Moses

*Do not practice homosexuality, having
sex with another man as with a woman.
It is a detestable sin.*[48]

The above scripture is abundantly clear. It is used consistently to demonstrate that God hates same-sex behavior. Because the text says God told this to Moses (and Moses simply wrote down what he heard), this is meant to provide God's unchanging opinion on this matter. It gives a sense of finality: "God said it. Case closed!"

But is that really the case?

It should be noted that many scholars believe that the Pentateuch (the first five books of the Hebrew Bible – which Christians call the Old Testament) were composed hundreds of years *after* Moses and were based on different historical traditions with different emphases. While the purpose of this book is not to get "into the weeds" on this topic, just keep in mind that scholars base their questions on archaeology, Hebrew grammar, and other considerations.

For the sake of this chapter, we will assume that what was written is as it happened, since many of my dear readers hold this more "conservative" view.

---

[48] Leviticus 18:22

The issue, then, is not whether it is in the Bible. Rather, it is whether a person who uses those verses so authoritatively is *consistent*, since there are a multitude of other verses where the instructions, according to the text, were given directly by God. If the verse at the beginning of this chapter still applies to us today (since it is "God's attitude"), then let's use this principle to see what else we must follow. [DISCLAIMER: The following list is provided purely for the sake of highlighting the importance of consistency and should not be interpreted as an endorsement.]

SABBATH

This is part of the "Big 10" written on stone by the finger of God himself. If you are not worshipping on Saturday, then you are disobedient to God's word.[49] Worshipping on Saturday is to last forever – so even changing the day of worship to Sunday is out![50] And capital punishment was proscribed for anyone who did not follow the Sabbath regulations![51]

---

[49] See, for example, Exodus, 20:8, 11; 31:13-16. 35:2
[50] Exodus 31:16
[51] Exodus 35:2

MIXED CLOTHING

"You must not wear clothing made of wool and linen woven together"[52]

Check your clothing labels and make sure you are not mixing cotton, linen, or (God forbid) polyester!

EXTREME DISCIPLINE

> *"Suppose a man has a stubborn and rebellious son who will not obey his father or mother, even though they discipline him. In such a case, the father and mother must take the son to the elders as they hold court at the town gate. The parents must say to the elders, this son of ours is stubborn and rebellious and refuses to obey. He is a glutton and a drunkard.' Then all the men of his town must stone him to death."*[53]

Harsh, but perhaps it cut down on discipline problems.

---

[52] Deuteronomy 22:11
[53] Deuteronomy 21:18-21

MARRY YOUR BROTHER'S WIFE

If a husband dies leaving his wife childless, the husband's brother was responsible for taking the widow as his wife[54] in hopes she would get pregnant, and the dead man would thus have a son to continue his family line. (This is the background of the wonderful love story in the Book of Ruth.) It is also a recipe for tension with two women (sometimes more) in the same household.

NO MORE SEAFOOD

That's right: no shrimp, lobster, oysters, scallops, mussels, clams. Catfish is also not allowed.[55]

NO MORE PORK

That includes pork chops, pork BBQ, pork rinds, pork sausage.[56]

SLAVERY
Slavery is supported in both the Old and New Testaments. There were regulations in place on how

---

[54] Even if he is already married and may have a family of his own.
[55] Deuteronomy 14:10
[56] Leviticus 11:4-8; 20:5; Deuteronomy 14:3-19

to treat Israelite slaves, when they could be released from slavery, the limited rights of enemy tribes who have been conquered in battle and now are slaves, etc. A slave who marries and has children has the possibility of eventually going free, but his wife and children would be slaves forever. The Israelites could buy slaves from neighboring countries only. If you are an American, that means any slave you buy must be from Canada or Mexico!

LEGALIZED SEX SLAVERY

On some occasions, when the Israelite army would fight and defeat another tribe or city, it was commanded that all the people be killed... except for young virgin daughters, who would be taken as slaves by the conquerors as spoils of war (and all that implies).[57]

USE A SHOVEL

When people needed to relieve themselves, they were to go to a quiet, secluded, private place, dig a hole, do their business, then cover up the hole, much like primitive camping in the forest today.[58] One can think how this ancient practice was necessary for

[57] Deuteronomy 21:10-14; Judges 21:8-14
[58] Deuteronomy 23:13

sanitation and reduced certain serious illnesses, and they would be right. It was much better than the chamber pots used in Europe in the Middle Ages where the contents were just tossed out the window into the street each day. And of course, nothing can beat modern sewage or septic systems. However, as silly as trying to replicate the ancient biblical practice is, it was the law of Moses spoken to him by God. If one truly wants to be consistent in following the Old Testament law, he or she better have a good camping shovel for daily use!

There are many activities that required the death penalty – various sexual sins, involvement in occult practices, idolatry, or blasphemy, to name a few.

To clarify, I am not endorsing any of these laws. I am simply saying that if one is going to use the trump card of "God told Moses" with one passage and that these laws are to last forever, that person should take the opportunity for introspection as to why the verse at the beginning of this chapter is emphasized while most of the others are not.

So, if one is going to use the verse at the beginning of the chapter to oppose homosexuality, then that person needs to be consistent and follow all the rest of Moses's commands, since they are all attributed to God. If certain commands, such as slavery or having multiple wives, are illegal in our current society, one should work to change state and federal laws, so people are free to conform to what God prescribed: free slave labor and polygamy!

As St. James declared,

> *For whosoever shall keep the*
> *whole law, and yet offend in one point,*
> *he is guilty of all.*[59]

I know some readers will say, "We're not under the Law of Moses anymore."

Yup!

"Christ fulfilled the Law and its requirements, so they no longer apply."

Uh-huh.

"We are not under Law, but under grace!"

True.

I, along with millions of other Christ-followers, affirm these statements. So how can one hold these beliefs while at the same time use a verse from the Law of Moses to condemn and exclude people whom God loves and welcomes?

---

[59] James 2:10

How do we reconcile these two opposing views?

The coming of Jesus.

Look at this amazing scripture:

> *No one has ever seen God. But the*
> *unique One, who is himself God, is near*
> *to the Father's heart. He has revealed*
> *God to us.*[60]

As I recounted in my book *A More Beautiful Faith – Seeing God Through the Eyes of Jesus*, the above verse was like a hand grenade blowing up my previous understanding of scripture.

Wow! No one has ever seen God – not Abraham, Moses, David, Elijah, Isaiah... That is a bold statement. Yet scripture records at least three of those men "saw" God! Perhaps we need another way to understand this verse.

To see something can mean seeing with one's physical eyes. But there is a more powerful meaning. When someone has a question and receives a reply that they comprehend, they often say, "Oh, I see!"

I believe this is what Jesus meant when he said:

> *God blesses those whose hearts are*
> *pure, for they will see God.*[61]

---

[60] John 1:18
[61] Matthew 5:8

He was not referring to going to heaven at death so one could see God. Rather, when our hearts are pure, we understand what God is like. When our hearts are free from prejudices, pride, fear, anger, resentment, we begin to perceive the heart of the God who is kind, welcoming, merciful, and caring to all.

Jesus taught that it was what comes out of the heart—hatred, lust, lying, etc.—that defiles a person, not the strict purification laws that religious folk hold so highly.

Jesus is the ultimate standard by which we can perceive what the Heavenly Father is like – not Moses, David, or any of the Hebrew prophets. He reveals the Father's heart toward people – especially the outcasts, those considered impure, and those rejected by organized religion.

Remember, based on the pure/impure list earlier in this book, most people Jesus healed were ceremonially unclean! And the fact that he touched them would make Jesus himself "unclean." The religious leaders considered him tainted because he kept going to dinner parties (sometimes inviting himself) with people who were considered outcasts by the respectable pious folk. Again, making him unclean.

When I think about those in the LGBTQ+ community who are stigmatized, ostracized, and rejected from so many "Bible believing" churches, I wonder with whom Jesus would identify.

In fact, I don't really wonder.

The one who perfectly demonstrated his Father's love would be hanging out with the outsiders, the rejected, the scorned.

And that, my friend, is good news!

CHAPTER 10 – Gotta Know Some History [For Mature Audiences Only]

"Don't know much about history..."[62]

High school history classes.

They were a snooze for many students who couldn't care less about what happened in years gone by. Trying to remember dates of wars, names of presidents, and different eras seemed to be completely irrelevant to modern life.

However, if one had great history teachers (which I had) plus was nerdy about such topics (which I was), history was fascinating and sometimes exciting. Living in Canada at the time, I loved the year we studied British history, all the way back to William the Conqueror, who conquered England in 1066 CE. While most of my classmates barely endured the course, I was engrossed with the drama of kings both good and bad, revolts from figures such as Oliver Cromwell, and the politics of great English statesmen like William Gladstone, Benjamin Disraeli, and Winston Churchill.

However, what significance does history hold for us in the present day?

Glad you asked.

---

[62] The first line from the song *Wonderful World* by Sam Cooke (1960).

History can be very pertinent when we approach ancient texts such as the Bible. Though it should seem obvious, many Bible readers forget that the Bible was not written to us in the 21st century. The languages, customs, and worldviews of the ancient biblical writers were in many ways totally different from our own. They faced challenges unknown to us. The opinions and advice given by the writers of the New Testament books—especially St. Paul—at times seem archaic and confusing. They can also be misunderstood and consequently misused by some Christian leaders to control their followers' behavior and to pronounce condemnation on those who do not comply.

Before we look at those passages, we must learn the historical context in which they were written. What you are about to read is not for the faint-at-heart or those easily offended. It is also definitely not appropriate for children. In fact, some of this was "toned down" for the more sensitive reader.

Roman Males' Sexual Practices

Being removed in time by two millennia, it is helpful to compare Roman society with North American society. There has been extensive research by historians on the sexual mores and practices of ancient Greece and Rome that are beyond the venue of this book. Philosophies such as Stoicism or

Epicureanism held different views on sexuality and public/private morals. However, below are some basic elements that were widely practiced and condoned. Our focus will be on Roman culture between 200 BCE and 200 CE:

- Roman society was very patriarchal compared to our own society (which is considered patriarchal by many today). Men—especially Roman citizens—dominated society, which also extended to sexual practices.
- Roman society was very class-conscious. There were those who were born as Roman citizens due to their parents' citizenship, and had many legal rights, including a right to a trial if accused of a crime. There were then those who managed to purchase Roman citizenship.[63] And then there was everyone else: the poor or slaves. The rights of non-citizens were very limited.
- Some sexual activities that are considered criminal today were common and not even frowned upon in ancient Roman society. Being a male Roman citizen in that culture gave the man a lot of sexual rights.
- Sex in our society, when at its best, is considered mutual gratification out of love

---

[63] An interesting passage in Acts 22:23-29, where St. Paul identifies himself as a Roman citizen by birth, while the battalion commander became a citizen by paying a lot of money.

and respect for the other partner. It could be the same at times in Roman society. For many, however, sex was also a sign of domination over an inferior figure.

The Horrible Practice of Pederasty

Most people today are not familiar with the term *pederasty*. It is basically the act of a man having sex with a boy. It was for the gratification and domination of the one doing the penetration and was legal and allowed if the young boy was not a "free Roman."

And it was not uncommon.

For example, a poor family who had little or no money to feed their children, would sell a prepubescent boy as a "servant" to a wealthier family. This young servant was not just used for cleaning the house and polishing the master's sandals like a rich man's valet. Sexual favors were implied as well. Sometimes the boy would be dressed as a girl and expected to act in "feminine" ways. As the boy went through puberty he became decreasingly desirable. He had to remain clean-shaven (which was considered a feminine trait.) By the time the boy was eighteen he would often be cast aside for a younger, more girlish boy. The older boy would end up on the streets and could only survive by becoming a male prostitute.

Beyond the "Clobber" Passages

Such activities are repulsive to our society, and rightly so. These behaviors are extremely damaging to the victims who sometimes carry the abuse with them for the rest of their lives. We consider it deviant criminal behavior and treat it accordingly in our justice system.

The Romans thought otherwise.

It was expected and socially acceptable for a freeborn Roman man to want sex with both female and male partners if he took the dominating role. Acceptable objects of desire were women of any social or legal status, male prostitutes, or male slaves, but sexual behaviors outside marriage were to be confined to slaves and prostitutes, or less often a concubine or "kept woman." Lack of self-control in managing one's sex life indicated that a man was incapable of governing others.[64]

The proper way for a Roman male to seek sexual gratification was to insert his penis in his partner. Allowing himself to be penetrated threatened his liberty as a free citizen as well as his sexual integrity.[65] This has been described as a "conquest mentality" or the Roman cult of "virility".

---

[64] Langlands, Rebecca. *Sexual morality in ancient Rome.* Cambridge University Press, 2006.
[65] Hallett, Judith P., and Marilyn B. Skinner, eds. Roman sexualities. Princeton University Press, 1997.

Sex at "Church"

The ancient Romans believed that the gods procreated with other gods and with humans. If it was OK for the gods to do that, then... well, you get the picture. Religion and sex were often blended. Many ancient temples had both male and female prostitutes as part of their 'liturgy'. Religious festivals often included sexual themes and practices. Here is a sample:

- *Lupercalia*, celebrated on February 15, focused on fertility. After a ceremony where goats or dogs were offered as sacrifices, the priests would skin the animals and cut the hides into long thin straps (called thongs). Young men would then take the thongs and run through the Palatine area of Rome. People (especially women) would line the route of the run (sort of like watching a 5K race.) If a runner struck a woman with the thong, that symbolized the god's blessing of fertility on the woman.

- *Floralia*, held in late April – early May, celebrated Flora, the goddess of flowers and spring, and included nude dancing. Prostitutes were celebrated. Instead of the common and appropriate Pastor Appreciation Day that thousands of modern churches observe each Autumn, this was Temple Prostitute Appreciation Week!

- Deities Cupid, Liber, and Venus had sexual aspects to their worship (including female and male prostitutes). Cupid and Liber were considered to inspire sexual desire and orgasms.

Effeminacy

Some readers may remember the old Saturday Night Live routines by Hans & Franz (played by Dana Carvey and Kevin Nealon respectively), two muscle-men with huge muscles in their arms, legs, and chest (with the aid of padded costumes, of course). They spoke with German accents and worshipped Arnold Schwarzenegger. One of their favorite insults was to call a weaker male a "girly mahn."

Some of my male readers no doubt experienced similar sneering insults as they grew up. Terms such as sissy, weakling, and other words inappropriate to say, were meant to mock and humiliate a guy deemed a weaker, inferior male.

Some things never change. Insulting a man's strength and masculinity was well-known in Rome, including insulting one's political opponent:

In the last years of the Republic, the popularists Julius Caesar, Marcus Antonius (Mark Antony), and Clodius Pulcher, as well as the Catilinarian conspirators, were all derided as effeminate, overly-groomed, too-good-looking men who might be on the receiving end of sex from other males; at the same time, they were supposed to be womanizers or possessed of devastating sex appeal.[66]

Effeminacy was a favorite accusation in Roman political invective, and was aimed particularly at... the politicians of the faction who represented themselves as champions of the people, sometimes called Rome's "democratic" party in contrast to the optimates, *a conservative elite of nobles.*[67]

> **"'Effeminacy' implied that the male was on the receiving end of sexual intercourse."**

It seems that insulting political opponents with obnoxious names is nothing new. But what is

---

[66] Edwards, Catharine. *The politics of immorality in ancient Rome.* Cambridge University Press, 2002.
[67] Ibid, pp. 63-64

fascinating is why being called effeminate was such a slur. If a man was clean-shaven, dressed well, and had sex appeal, he might qualify as effeminate! That would include most of our slicker politicians and many Christian leaders and TV preachers (but I digress). But in the Roman context, as seen above, effeminacy implied that, because the male is on the receiving end of sexual intercourse, he is weaker and inferior to other men. "Effeminacy" implied that the male was on the receiving end of sexual intercourse.

A Little Greek is Good for You (I mean a Greek word, not a pita sandwich)

St. Paul wrote his letters in ancient Greek. Translators of ancient languages sometimes add interpretations, which helps modern readers understand the text better. Sometimes, however, interpretations can go too far based perhaps on the bias and/or beliefs of the translator.

A great example of this is in 1 Corinthians 6:9-11, where Paul lists several activities that disqualify a person from the "kingdom of God." One Greek word on that list is *malakos* (pronounced mal-a-KOS). It means soft or soft to the touch – such as soft skin or soft clothing – and by implication has been translated as *effeminate.* Some Bible versions translate the word as "homosexual," which modern readers equate with the gay community in general. However, the ancient meaning of *malakos* was much more nuanced. The term could be used euphemistically to describe a boy kept for homosexual relations; a male on the receiving end of a male sexual encounter; or a male prostitute (in ancient parlance called a "catamite."). It seems to me that these examples are *victims* of sexual aggression, not perpetrators. Perhaps any condemnation should be toward those who exploit weaker people for their own gratification and sense of superiority.

Why Is This Important?

As I mentioned at the beginning of this chapter, historical context is needed when dealing with ancient texts such as the Bible. In the next chapter, we will look at another scripture in the New Testament that has been used to condemn people in the gay community. On the surface, those verses seem cut-and-dry. But in *historical context*, they may take on a different meaning.

CHAPTER 11 – The Stone of Paul

Fool's Gold.

When I was a boy, our family would drive to visit my grandparents in northern Minnesota. Their small home was located on a gravel/dirt road many miles from the nearest town. Because there was not much to occupy the time of my younger sister and me, we would walk up and down the road looking for "precious" rocks - meaning any stones such as agates, quartz, and even granite.

One day I happened to find a small stone that looked like a piece of coral but contained tiny chunks of something that looked like gold. Ecstatic, I could imagine myself now striking it rich, buying a new bicycle and some new comic books, not to mention a princely trip to the candy store when I got home. If I had been allowed to watch the James Bond movie *Goldfinger*, I am sure I would have been humming the title song all the way back to my grandparents' house.

Imagine my disappointment when I learned from my grandparents that I was holding in my hand fool's gold, a mostly worthless rock made from pyrite (also known as iron sulfide). My dreams of being the world's youngest gold baron were shattered!

Striking it "rich" with Bible verses

Not understanding the historical context of Bible verses and thus misusing or misapplying those verses can become the theological version of fool's gold. We may think we have struck gold with a few verses but in fact our interpretation is only a cheap imitation. I again emphasize that I am not disparaging the Bible. Rather, I am critiquing our methods of interpretation that allow us to use Bible verses to "stone" our victims.

Bible verses can be used to shame and condemn gays and lesbians, driving them from the church and poisoning the possibility of discovering the love of God for themselves. Here is one of the most-used passages from the New Testament:

> *That is why God abandoned them to their shameful desires. Even the women turned against the natural way to have sex and instead indulged in sex with each other. And the men, instead of having normal sexual relations with women, burned with lust for each other. Men did shameful things with other men, and as a result of this sin, they suffered within themselves the penalty they deserved.*[68]

------

[68] Romans 1:26-27

These two Bible verses seem brutally clear. And, though taken out of context, they have become "proof texts" to demonstrate how God hates homosexuals and has abandoned them. And, to add insult to injury, homosexuality itself is deemed the judgment on individuals by a wrathful God.

But to what is this passage referring?

Gotta know some history!

Remember the little history lesson in our last chapter on sexual practices in ancient Rome? How the temples of their gods had male and female prostitutes? How some of their religious holidays contained nudity, with sex between males as well as females? This was part of the cultural and religious milieu of the day.

Let's take the two verses quoted above and put them back into context. In Romans 1:18, St. Paul begins a diatribe against pagan idolatry, going back in history as to why the gods were "invented," and what happened when people rejected knowledge of the true God. God's judgment was to abandon the idol worshippers and let them do whatever they wanted, which included same-gender sex. The result was not, as some would suggest, burning in hellfire forever, but rather the negative impact within the person committing the acts: *they suffered **within themselves** the penalty they deserved.*

In this specific context Paul is talking about idol worship and sex. It could be expanded beyond their worship liturgy, as we have seen, to the broader culture of heterosexual men choosing pederasty, sex with women (besides their spouses) or men, both for pleasure and to demonstrate domination.

There is no historical evidence that the ancients understood sexual orientation in the modern sense, in which scientific research continues to identify certain chromosomes as well as influences outside the mother's body that help steer someone toward a specific sexual orientation. For the ancients, what we would call bisexuality was simply men being men.

Three more insights.

Paul refers to *natural* sexual activity - meaning between male and female - and by implication *unnatural* sexual activity (same sex). Along with his Jewish culture, he saw natural activity as defined by body parts. However, in our time, due to great advances in science and genomics, our criteria for what is natural is based on hormones and chemistry.[69] This has huge implications when considering individuals who truthfully say they born with gay tendencies.

Secondly, Paul refers to same-sex activity as a *result* of the wrath of God, giving people over to their idolatry. But Paul does not stop there; here is a list of sixteen(!) other behaviors/attitudes that God in his wrath abandoned people to do:[70]

---

[69] This insight came from John Dominic Crossan in his book, *God and Empire*, HarperCollins, 2007)
[70] Romans 1:29-31

Wickedness & sin	Deception
Greed	Gossip
Hate	Malicious behavior
Envy	Backstabbers
Murder	Haters of God
Quarreling	Proud and boastful
Disobedient to parents	Promise-breakers
Heartless	Merciless

Having been raised in church and spending much of my adult life serving in various ministry capacities, I have probably seen everything on the above list done except murder – and that's in a church environment! It is amazing to me (though not necessarily surprising) that same-gender relationships are angrily and loudly preached against, yet I have heard little or no teaching about envy, quarreling, pride, keeping our word, showing mercy, not gossiping, not being two-faced. And all these attitudes and actions are included as God's judgment on idolatrous humans. Which means that anyone who does any of the above list is just as guilty as if they had sex with a temple prostitute! Ouch!

Second, Paul's point continues in chapter two of Romans.[71] Look at this fun verse:

---

[71] Remember there were no chapters or verses in the original writings, so Paul is just continuing his thought from Romans 1.

You may think you can condemn such people, but you are just as bad, and you have no excuse! When you say they are wicked and should be punished, you are condemning yourself, for you who judge others do these very same things. [72]

As with many other topics, Christians have turned these verses into an adventure in missing the point. So much vitriol and condemnation of one behavior while ignoring or denying sixteen others! If I recall, Jesus said something about getting a log out of our eye before we go after the splinter in another. [73] Paul's argument ultimately leads up to the famous Bible verse that Christians like to quote: "For *all* have sinned and come short of the glory of God." [74]

Maybe the above verses could be summarized in the old maxim, "People in glass houses shouldn't throw stones."

Finally, the activities Paul witnessed in an idol-infested culture that celebrated various sexual practices in its worship do not so easily apply to many people today. Think of those raised in Christian homes and who became Christians at an early age. They love Jesus. They have never been involved in idolatry. And yet the wrath of God is on

---

[72] Romans 2:1
[73] Matthew 7:3
[74] Romans 3:23 – King James Version

them because they were born with a same-sex attraction?

I don't think so.

It is bad enough that those who are not Christ-followers are often condemned by much of the church – especially when it comes to same-sex relationships. But to condemn those who have faithfully loved and served the Lord but have a same-sex orientation is appalling and horrendous.

It is also disingenuous to single out one behavior on the list, use that to condemn others, and de-emphasize or ignore all the other activities that are equally as bad! I believe the word that Jesus used to describe such people was *hypocrites*.

We are all guilty of hypocrisy.

But as any recovering addict will tell us, the first step out of addiction is to acknowledge the problem and realize we need outside help to change. In our case, what is the root problem? What fuels our hypocrisy? In acknowledging the root causes, we can find healing. We will discuss this later.......

There is one more stone, however, I want to address.

CHAPTER 12 – The Stone of Rejection

"We Don't Need You!"

The eye can never say to the hand, "I don't need you." The head can't say to the feet, "I don't need you." In fact, some parts of the body that seem weakest and least important are actually the most necessary.[75]

Years ago, when my wife and I needed a break from ministry responsibilities, we searched for a large church where we could remain anonymous – just attend, put some money in the offering plate, and slip out at the end of the service. (That can't be done in a smaller congregation, who notices visitors right away and is quick to discover if those visitors have abilities that are needed. I think I've heard the silent but still very evident words from them, "Ah, fresh meat!" But I digress.)

Anyway, we found a large church in the city we were living in at the time. The pastor was what I would call a southern "good ol' boy." I don't mean that in a pejorative sense. He was not a "hellfire, spit and holler" preacher. Rather, he was basically a down-to-earth Bible teacher with a southern drawl

---

[75] 1 Corinthians 12:21-22

who had a laid-back personal charisma that drew hundreds to him.

One of the things that attracted us to the church, however, was the music. They had a dynamic choir and a lot of outstanding soloists and instrumentalists, which is common in very large congregations. But what was evident to me was that the music was so vibrant because of the minister of music. He was a younger man, probably in his mid-thirties. He could obviously play piano very well and sing – but there was more. We could sense he had a distinct "ability."

Let me explain.

There are many excellent musicians in the world today. Often, they have been trained in the best conservatories or universities. They are extraordinarily talented and many of them have gone on to have huge careers in music. There are others, though talented and trained, who may not be at the same musical level as the others I just described. But what sets them apart is this special ability. When they sing, play an instrument, or lead a choir, something happens in the room. The atmosphere changes. It seems to be charged with holy energy. People can feel it. The responses vary – some may begin to quietly weep, others may look up with raised hands, quietly worshipping the Lord. Sometimes, once the music is through, there is a holy hush in the room – no talking, singing, or applause. It feels like if one even moves or sneezes, they could ruin the moment, because it feels so holy, so special. One of the Hebrew prophets described it this way:

> *But the LORD is in his holy Temple.*
> *Let all the earth be silent before him.*[76]

This atmosphere is not the same as using emotional manipulation, dimming the auditorium lights, or turning on a fog machine, as happens in some churches. This ability seems to come from somewhere else.[77] One feels like they are having an encounter with the living God.

But back to my story.

We never personally met the music minister (remember we were trying to stay anonymous) but we were impressed with both his talent and this special gift that God had given him for the job.

We eventually moved from that city to another state. A few months later, I called a friend of mine who still lived in the area and asked how things were going at that church. He told me the music minister, whom we had appreciated so much, had been quietly removed from his position.

The reason?

It was discovered that he was gay.

---

[76] Habakkuk 2:20

[77] Whether or not that is technically true theologically, I am simply describing the *experience* of the anointing that I have encountered many times over the years.

Think about that.

Someone with talents given to him by God, someone who deeply loved the Lord and was accepted by him, someone who knew how to lead a thousand people in dynamic

"Rejection breeds rejection."

worship (it was obvious he was a worshipper, too), someone who was given a special ability from the Holy Spirit...

Was fired because of his sexual orientation.

Sadly, this story is not uncommon in many churches across the country, and they are the poorer for it. One gay man told me that, when he went to karaoke clubs that catered to the gay population, it was amazing how many of the clientele knew so many Christian songs and hymns.

Why?

Because until they were rejected by their churches, whether through condemning sermons, congregational attitudes, or perhaps even being fired from a leadership position or were asked to leave, had been raised in, served in, participated in that church.

"We don't need you!"

So many Christians wring their hands and fret when they see news reports of militant LGBTQ+ groups marching in the streets, defiantly rejecting organized religion – especially Christianity. "A sign of the end times," some will lament.

But what should one expect? Rejection breeds rejection. When Christians judge, condemn, and reject their fellow humans based on a small trickle of Bible verses taken out of context, they should not be surprised when the victims reject them! The irony is that many Christians feel they are being persecuted by society for their beliefs about these matters, when in fact they are simply reaping what they sowed!

What difference might it have made had churches shown kindness, true acceptance, and full inclusion into the life of the church? How many more from the LGBTQ+ community might be faithful Jesus-followers today? How many churches would be enriched by the valuable and needed talents, resources, and personalities of these wonderful people?

Remember St. Paul's analogy from the beginning of this chapter.

The eye needs to say to the hand, "I need you! This whole body needs your manual dexterity!" The hand needs to reply to the eye, "Your sight provides me direction so I can accomplish my tasks! I need you!"

The head must declare to the feet, "I need you! I can't walk anywhere without you!" The feet must respond, "I need that brain inside your head for muscle coordination and direction. I desperately need you!"

Beyond the "Clobber" Passages

It is easy to forget that we are all interconnected. We need each other to come to completeness — mentally, emotionally, and spiritually.

And that includes those in the LGBTQ+ community.

CHAPTER 13 – Stop the Stoning!

The story of Leah in chapter six is based on the first eight verses in the Gospel of John, chapter eight. It is one of the most famous episodes in the life of Christ. Ironically, that story is not in the most ancient manuscripts. No matter who inserted it into the text, it certainly fits the narrative of how Jesus interacted with those considered sinners. When one reads the four gospels, there is episode after episode of Jesus receiving, forgiving, accepting, and loving those condemned by the more pious folk. Indeed, he reserved his greatest denunciations for those who used scriptures to control, exclude, and harm others.

Thankfully, stoning is illegal in western countries today. In the annals of capital punishment, it was one of the most inhumane and tortuous ways to kill a person. While an arrow (or bullet), a beheading, an electric chair, or lethal injection can be quick to do their job, pitching softball-size or larger stones at a victim amounts to a slower, more painful death. Crucifixion is perhaps one of the only methods that is more prolonged and excruciating.

So stoning is out.

Or is it?

There are so many ways to stone people without throwing actual rocks. Sadly, scripture verses have often been used as stones to condemn and exclude others - even including violence. Here are some examples from the last few centuries:

> The slaughter and/or subjugation of aboriginal peoples in North America and around the world, justifying it by the model of the Hebrew nation taking over the land of Israel in the Book of Joshua.
> The support and practice of slavery.
> Limiting women's roles in society, leadership, and in church ministry; controlling a woman's looks: hair length, wearing of jewelry and make-up; total submission of a woman to her father or husband.
> Divorce and remarriage without consideration for infidelity, abandonment, or abuse, by one's partner.
> Hippies and other countercultural groups (see the movie *Jesus Revolution* for examples)
> The LGBTQ+ community

Once again, I am not criticizing the Bible. I am, however, critiquing the way it has been interpreted and applied that causes so much pain to so many.

The Heart Transplant Specialist

As I noted earlier in this book, when I discuss with others the implications of the story of Leah in chapter six, their main "take-away" often is that Jesus told her not to sin again. It is almost always interpreted as Jesus issuing a divine threat, "You got away with it this time, but next time you won't be so lucky!"

The deeper problem is that a part of human nature is to gather stones to throw rather than garments to cover; to deflect or project our prejudices and judgments onto others instead of much-needed introspection.

To use a metaphor from the Old Testament, we have stony hearts – hearts of stone – rather than hearts of flesh. And out of the abundance of our hearts come pride, anger, rage, and judgment. People with soft hearts do not throw hard stones! Using proof texts from scripture does not alter the fact that many of us have cold, rigid hearts.

But there is good news! God promises a heart transplant!

> *And I will give you a new heart, and I will put a new spirit in you. I will take out your stony, stubborn heart and give you a tender, responsive heart.*[78]

---

[78] Ezekiel 36:26

So be encouraged, my dear friend. If you are sensing a growing love and acceptance toward others whom you once considered to

"People with soft hearts do not throw hard stones!"

be in the depths of sin, whether it is someone from a different religion, a political party, or sexual orientation, you are experiencing a gradual heart transplant from your loving Heavenly Father. Elsewhere the Bible defines this as "growing in grace."[79] When someone else begins to throw stones, even if the stones are hand-picked Bible verses, you will intuitively know that what they are saying – even if they use the Bible – does not sound like your Heavenly Father or the Lord Jesus.

If that has not been your experience so far, be intentional in asking the Master to reveal his heart and attitudes to you and help you change your thinking.

It is a request he loves to answer.

---

[79] 2 Peter 3:18

CHAPTER 14 – The Phone Call

Our lives all have their twists and turns. I have experienced several. This true story is to give my readers context into an important change that thirty years ago I would never have imagined.

But first, some background.

As mentioned earlier, I was raised in a pastor's home and have been a Christ-follower most of my life. Because of my parents' dedication to helping me develop my talents, over time I became an accomplished pianist, choral director, and music arranger. Over my career I served on church staffs (large & small) as Associate Pastor/Minister of Music, plus pastored my own church for 10 years.

I am a straight white male.

From childhood through college, I did not know anyone who was gay.

Well, that is only partially true.

I had a few dear friends who were gay, but I didn't know it then. Being Christians themselves and attending the same conservative evangelical colleges and churches I did, they dared not reveal their sexual orientation lest they be disfellowshipped and be asked to leave. Being raised in a very conservative environment, I embraced our religious community's belief that homosexuality was a horrible sin (even for celibate gays.) It wasn't really discussed in sermons or Bible studies as it would not become an "issue" until a few years later. It was just the way we believed, based on a handful of Bible verses (which we have already addressed in previous chapters.)

The Brunch That Started It All

I was associate pastor in a mid-sized church in the American southwest. We had two services each Sunday morning with a two-hour gap between them. One Sunday one of the leaders in the church and I decided to go get some brunch at a local restaurant. It was known by that church that he had previously been part of the "gay lifestyle" and all that entails, but was, to my knowledge at the time, living a celibate life.

During the meal I asked him to tell me his story. He discussed being raised in a Pentecostal church, and by the time he was a teenager he knew he was gay. He eventually left the church, moved to a large city, and became part of the "gay scene," with all the activities that are commonly associated with that way of life. While I was inwardly uncomfortable by some of his stories (but trying not to let it show), I sensed there was a lot of pain and self-rejection. He told me he had tried to change, begged God to change him, and tried unsuccessfully to not be how he was born. While it would take years for my thinking to evolve on this topic, I felt empathy for him and did not condemn him in any way.

I had already experienced just a sliver of what gays deal with in the average conservative church. A few years previously I served on the pastoral staff of a large church in the south. We had many good friends in that congregation, but there was one couple with whom my wife and I were very close. They were two of the most delightful friends we ever had! He had a riotous and wicked sense of humor, and we would laugh hilariously at the stories of some of the ridiculous situations they found themselves in. We enjoyed hanging out with them regularly. They loved Jesus but there was no religiosity in their beings!

Our friendship, however, caused some suspicion about me.

Let me explain.

Our friend was suspected to be a closet gay (he was gay,) though he didn't come out until sometime later.) The pastor for whom I worked was somewhat suspicious that I might be gay – the *only* evidence being that we were friends with the couple, and I considered the husband a great guy. It was a "birds of a feather flock together" type of subtle accusation. My only "sin" was that I was a good friend. I realized at the time how our beliefs can make us closed-minded and quick to judge.

Still, while I eventually became senior pastor of a wonderful church, my attitudes were slow to evolve. I remember one sermon where the subject of homosexuality came up and I used the line I had

117

stolen from someone else (I don't remember who), "God made Adam and Eve, not Adam and Steve!" Though many in the congregation laughed at the time, I knew intuitively that my glib remark had wounded someone. I didn't know who it was, since I didn't know that anyone in the church might be gay. But I knew what I said was wrong.

My heart slowly started to sense more compassion for people who come to church needing healing, support, and a safe space without rejection only to be mocked for their internal pain.

I knew things were changing when sometime later we had a guest minister at our church. She was nationally known, and we were honored that she loved preaching at our church – she had been there several times. This time, however, it was different. During the sermon, her countenance changed. Her delivery became fiery; her face became beet-red, and she started preaching against homosexuals with strong intensity, using the term "fag" in her sermon. Perhaps years before I would have smiled and nodded in agreement. This time, though, it felt like a gut punch! My understanding of scripture had yet to evolve, but I strongly knew intuitively that what she was preaching-–-and the way she was delivering it-–-was not of God.

Little did I know at the time that God was preparing me for something closer to home.

The Phone Call

One afternoon several years later, we were living in another state.

As any parent with more than one child knows, kids can be raised in the same household, be loved and treated the same, but can turn out as different as night and day. It's the way they were born. We have four grown sons and one daughter. They all love Jesus and have turned out to be wonderful adults (in my totally unbiased opinion.) However, no two of them are alike.

We noticed early on that one of our sons wasn't as interested in the usual "boy" stuff – he wasn't as rough and tumble as his brothers. He didn't care for toy cars, building sets, and activities that boys typically enjoy doing. He had different sensibilities and interests. He had a great personality, was fun and outgoing, and could be a tad dramatic at times. He cared about his appearance much more than his brothers cared for theirs.[80]

In high school he had several female friends but no girlfriend. He excelled in school and was a natural leader. During that time, he went on several mission trips to Mexico, Venezuela, Russia, Nepal, and China.

---

[80] I tell this story with my son's full permission, as I would not write anything that would embarrass or hurt him.

After finishing his undergraduate studies in university, he did a successful stint in the army, serving both in the U.S. and overseas.

Then came the phone call.

"Dad, there's something I have to tell you."

"Sure, what is it?"

"I've realized that I am gay, and I am coming out."

To be honest, it was a relief, as his mother and I had suspected this since his early childhood, but in our frame of mind at that time in his life we didn't want to say or do anything to either shame him or encourage him.

When he admitted to me that he was gay, I was able to reply, "Son, I'm not disappointed *in* you; I'm disappointed *for* you. I know that being gay in our society is not going to be easy. Mom and I aren't really surprised, but I want you to know that we love you and are standing with you."

He later told me that this is what he thought I would say. I was so thankful the Lord had prepared my heart and mind so I would not have to face the dilemma that many Christian parents must face — do they love and support their son or daughter or stand firm in their religious beliefs, even if it means alienating their child? Questions arise, such as, "If we support our child, what will our pastor and Christian friends think? Will we become pariahs in our congregation? Will we lose our friends or family members who will judge us as compromising our values? And worst of all, will God reject us for disobedience and not standing for 'holiness'?

These are common concerns that Christians in fundamentalist/conservative churches struggle with today. I strongly believed, and still do, that our attitude was the right one, even though it caused tension with some of our friends and family.

No matter.

Jesus, quoting the Hebrew prophet Hosea, told the religious crowd:

> *Now go and learn the meaning of this Scripture: 'I* [Yahweh] *want you to show mercy, not offer sacrifices.'* [81]

I have learned that showing kindness, mercy, and support is more important to God than sacrificing loving relationships to stay loyal to one's interpretation of a few Bible verses.

One reason I tell this story is that some readers may think that I just changed my beliefs so I could accept my son's announcement. That was not the case at all. As I stated above, God was working in my heart long before that phone call. I was still aware of the "stone verses" against homosexuality in the Bible and had used them myself as a bludgeon on more than one occasion. I was learning, however, that when we experience God doing something in our

---

[81] Hosea 6:6; Matthew 9:13

hearts, sometimes it takes time for the mind to catch up.

St. Paul understood the need for updated thinking when he wrote:

> ... *let God transform you into **a new person by changing the way you think**. Then you will learn to know God's will for you, which is good and pleasing and perfect.*[82] [Empasis mine]

If you, dear reader, are struggling or know someone who is struggling with this or other "hot button" issues, then keep reading. I hope to give a fresh perspective on how to better handle the "clobber" verses, plus walk together on a new path to better know the kindness, love, and welcoming nature of God.

---

[82] Romans 12:2b

CHAPTER 15 – The Beautiful People at the Party

During these last two chapters, I want to reflect on the story of the world's richest man's party in chapter one. But first, take a moment to carefully read one of the most beautiful passages in scripture:

> *Thank you for making me so wonderfully complex!*
> *Your workmanship is marvelous—how well I know it.*
> *You watched me as I was being formed in utter seclusion,*
> *as I was woven together in the dark of the womb.*
> *You saw me before I was born.*
> *Every day of my life was recorded in your book.*
> *Every moment was laid out before a single day had passed.*
> *How precious are your thoughts about me, O God.*
> *They cannot be numbered!*[83]

---

[83] Psalm 139:14-17

This beautiful ancient poem, attributed to King David in the Hebrew Bible, inspires awe and gratefulness in those who meditate on its meaning. Though the author was talking about himself, millions of people intuitively believe that it describes their experience with God, even in utero.

But some will respond, "Aren't we each a product of a sperm and egg uniting, tying together multiple strands of DNA? Doesn't the environment in which the mother and fetus exist have an impact? Lack of a proper diet, trauma, stress – don't they play a part?"

All true.

But having to choose between human anatomy and the influence of God is a false choice. Why can't both be true in their own way? At its best, the Bible describes God as being everywhere all at once. Earlier in the poem quoted above, it reads:

> *I can never escape from your Spirit!*
> *I can never get away from your*
> *presence!*
> *If I go up to heaven, you are there;*
> *if I go down to the grave, you are there.*
> *If I ride the wings of the morning,*
> *if I dwell by the farthest oceans,*
> *even there your hand will guide me,*
> *and your strength will support me.*

I could ask the darkness to hide me
and the light around me to become
night—
but even in darkness I cannot hide
from you.
To you the night shines as bright as
day.
Darkness and light are the same to
you.[84]

The New Testament describes the same thing:

[Christ] is all, and in all.[85]

If God and Christ are present everywhere, as the scriptures above assert, then in some sense they are indeed aware of what goes on in a woman's womb and the forming of the fetus. And somehow there is delight and love for the baby growing inside her. Even if the baby isn't "perfect" – perhaps with a deformity or disease of some kind – there is an immense love of God, who loves all things and all people, even with our imperfections, whatever they may be.

So what does this have to do with the topic of this book?

Great question! Glad you asked.

---

[84] Psalm 139:7-12
[85] Colossians 3:11

One of the most common themes when I talk to those who are gay is their conviction that they were born that way. It was not a personal choice, like choosing a meal from a restaurant menu or deciding which brand of car to purchase. None of them said, "I woke up one morning and decided I *want* to be a homosexual." A friend described the hard struggle being gay in our society, including the rejection of family and friends once he was outed, and the shame and condemnation he heard at churches he visited. Those who were raised in many evangelical or fundamentalist churches also carried the stigma of being hated by God, who judged them by letting them be gay due to some perceived sin (á la Romans 1). As one said to me with tears in his eyes, "I would never choose to be gay."

I asked him why some heterosexual men so strongly insist that being gay is a choice. His response was fascinating. Based on his observations, my friend believes that such a strong reaction derives from that person who at one time, perhaps during puberty and for whatever reason, questioned their own sexual orientation. That individual finally determined that he was *not* gay, and if he could choose not to be, it was the same for everyone else.

To whatever extent and by whatever factors sexual orientation is formed in the womb, according to scripture, that person is the workmanship of wonderful complexity by a God who sees him as precious (see the quote at the beginning of this chapter).

And finally, a loving challenge to my many friends who are "pro-life." The passage quoted at the beginning of this chapter is used by pro-life groups to say all life within the mother's womb is precious, that it is a gift designed by God. Even though we know that DNA and other factors help determine what the fetus will become, somehow God is involved in the process.

It doesn't matter if the baby is a boy or a girl, if it has red hair or brown eyes, if it looks like its mother or its father (even if the dad does not have 'movie star' good looks); it doesn't matter if the baby has some physical deformity or is sickly. In all these cases, the baby is cherished by the God of love and is treasured.

And I agree.

So… isn't it time to see those who have been born gay as being formed in the womb by a loving God who delights in each of them as well?

Just sayin'…

CHAPTER 16 – The God of Hospitality

Like the billionaire in chapter one who invited everyone in his town–no matter their wealth, social status, or ability to repay the favor–God is hospitable to all of us, no matter our race, gender, politics, nationality, or sexual orientation.

> *For God was in Christ, reconciling the world to himself, no longer counting people's sins against them. And he gave us this wonderful message of reconciliation. So we are Christ's ambassadors; God is making his appeal through us. We speak for Christ when we plead, "Come back to God!"*[86]

My friends, this is great news!

What I am going to say is not to impugn anyone's motives. I believe most Christians and their pastors are sincere and trying to follow Christ as best they know how. This is more an observation of the message that is emphasized.

So many Christians and churches seem stuck on a "John the Baptist" message – repent of your sins, live right, judgment is coming. That's not necessarily

---

[86] 2 Corinthians 5:19-20

a bad message but remember that John the Baptist's work was *before* the revelation of Jesus Christ!

Re-read the above verses.

The crucifixion of Christ was a reconciling act – not that God needed to change his attitude about us as some teach, but to change our attitude about God. Those two verses sum up the gospel:

The whole world—everyone—has been reconciled to God already. God is not counting our sins against us.

God is not angry with you.

God does not despise you.

God is not disgusted with you.

From his perspective, he has always been reconciled to you. All sins—past, present, future—are forgiven.

And if the good news of Christ means anything, it is an invitation to establish or re-establish a deep relationship with God, because he loves you, likes you (after all you are part of his *good* creation[87]), and be welcomed to his party.

What a beautiful message this is!

So many of us have lived under a "baptism of John" message, emphasizing holy living (as variously defined), criticism of and separation from people who do not conform to our standards, even if they are Christians themselves, and waiting for the Lord to judge all sinners. Again, I am not attacking

---

[87] Genesis 1:31

anyone's sincerity or love of the Lord. I just believe there is a better, more joyful message: Christ *has* come, the world *has been* reconciled to God the Father, our sins are *already* forgiven.

> *But as people sinned more and more,*
> *God's wonderful grace became more*
> *abundant.*[88]

Or to those who are more familiar with the old King James version, "Where sin abounded, grace did much more abound."

The Skunk

Years ago, we had a wonderful golden retriever named Princess – a beautiful, exuberant family dog. One day, for whatever reason (except perhaps that she was simply a dog being a dog), Princess decided to explore the south end of a skunk.

It did not end well.

We can attest that skunks have a long-range, powerful projectile weapon that shoots from their hind quarters! The skunk sprayed Princess's face, including her eyes and mouth, as well as her beautiful golden coat on both sides of her body. When Princess returned to our house, she was sick

---

88 Romans 5:20b

(swallowing skunk 'perfume' tends to do that), eyes watering, and horribly malodorous! She was sprayed with a hose, then given a bath with strong soap, then washed with tomato juice, which is also supposed to help remove the skunk odor. She was also encouraged to spend much more time in our fenced backyard.

It was all only of moderate help.

Everywhere she went in the house, the skunk bouquet travelled with her. It took days for the stench to fade away on both Princess and in the house.

Recently, one of my sons related to me that Princess loved to come into his bedroom every morning, lick his face and breathe on him, all to get him out of bed. It became a daily reminder that Princess had skunk breath. (And it was a stinky but effective 'alarm clock'!)

One evidence that I know God must really love my wife and me is that at the time of this skunk episode, she and I were hundreds of miles away at a conference in Washington, D.C. Our kids, as well as the couple who had agreed to stay with them in our absence, got the 'honor' of skunk duty.

Why this story?

There is a religious phrase that so many people use that, though they may not realize it, is the religious version of skunk spray. To be charitable, I believe that many sincerely use this concept to try to be true both to the Bible and to those whose behavior they reject.

It is generally unworkable.

When someone says that they "hate-the-sin-but-love-the-sinner," what invariably lingers is the first of those seven words: hate. Not "I-hate-you-and-want-to-murder-you" kind of hate, but a much softer but very real conditional acceptance that may communicate what the person really means: "I'm trying to love you, even though I believe that God is disgusted with you and will probably send you to hell anyway for your egregious sinning."

If a person deeply believes, based on a very few verses in scripture taken out of context, that God loves-yet-hates those who are not heterosexual and has given them a one-way ticket to hell, then the best that can happen is for that Christian to try to be "loving" in a superficial way.

Which brings me to a deeper point.

Often Christians respond to these issues based on their view of God. If God hates something or someone (especially as sometimes stated in the Hebrew scriptures), and we want to be like God, then perhaps "hate-the-sin-but-love-the-sinner" is the best one can do.

As I pointed out repeatedly in my book *A More Beautiful Faith*, the blind spot so many Christians and their spiritual leaders have is that if you really want to know what the Heavenly Father is like, you must look at Jesus – not Moses, not Joshua, not the prophets, not the history books that describe God encouraging genocide, capital punishment for various and sundry infractions, and his general distaste for his creation (such as the flood story.)[89] Yes, all those are in our sacred scriptures, but they are trumped by something much greater – the coming of Jesus!

> *No one has ever seen God. But the unique One, who is himself God, is near to the Father's heart. He has revealed God to us.*[90]

Though I said this earlier, it is worth repeating. No one has ever seen God. What a strong statement! Though the Bible describes Moses, Isaiah, Daniel, and others who experienced visions of God, "seeing" God is much more than a visual experience. It means understanding God, as when a person explains something to another and he/she replies, "Oh, now I see what you're saying."

As brilliant as Moses and the prophets were, they still understood God in a much more limited capacity.

It is not their fault.

They did the best with what they had.

But they did not have the revelation of the Father as seen through Jesus.

---

[89] Genesis 6-8
[90] John 1:18

> *For the law was given through Moses, but God's unfailing love and faithfulness came through Jesus Christ.*[91]

Note the emphasis on the above verse: Moses wrote the law--the rules, the decrees, the protocols--and believed that God dictated them to him.

But what did Jesus reveal to us?

God's unfailing love and faithfulness.

As radical an idea as this is for so many who have a great love of scripture (as I do), we must take this one step further. When the descriptions of the loving Father as revealed by Jesus contradict the pictures of God in other places of scripture, *Jesus must always take precedent*. If one feels the need to "balance" Jesus' teachings with contradictory statements in other parts of the Bible, two things happen:

1. Jesus always loses. I have often observed that this happens because Jesus' teachings seem "impractical" and not as personally satisfying as seeing people punished and having our own fears and prejudices affirmed by Bible verses.

2. Though unintentionally, one is implying that the teachings and examples of Jesus are no

---

[91] John 1:17

more than equal value to everything else. If Jesus is just another prophet in the mold of Moses and Elijah, that would probably be OK. But if he is the Son of God, truly revealing the heart of the Father from whom he came, as Christians assert, then that "balancing" act borders on denying the value of the Savior we claim to love!

So, instead of taking a "hate-the-sin-but-love-the-sinner" approach, perhaps it is time to develop a different attitude as taught by Jesus:

> *Do not judge others, and you will not be judged. For you will be treated as you treat others. The standard you use in judging is the standard by which you will be judged. And why worry about a speck in your friend's eye when you have a log in your own? How can you think of saying to your friend, 'Let me help you get rid of that speck in your eye,' when you can't see past the log in your own eye? Hypocrite! First get rid of the log in your own eye; then you will see well enough to deal with the speck in your friend's eye.*[92]

---

[92] Matthew 7:1-5

As discussed in chapter eleven, St. Paul used this same argument when he listed a large variety of sins that idol worshippers commit and then turns the table on his readers and declares they do the same things!

Several years ago, I heard a preacher succinctly sum up the above five verses in one sentence: *love others and hate your own damn sin!*

Great advice, even if it is a little crude.

Trust the Holy Spirit

I understand how this message gives some Christians extreme indigestion. Questions instantly arise, "But what about repenting from sinful activities? What about being holy in our thoughts and actions? How are people going to do what's right if we don't emphasize the need to not sin?" (Of course, people's definition of "sin" is often varied, but I digress.)

As you may have detected throughout this book, I do not think that homosexuality is necessarily a sin. As with heterosexual practices, some activities may be wrong if they harm another person, are not consensual, or are done to show domination over the other. None of that, whether gay or straight, is in line with the character or ethics of Jesus.

But, for the sake of argument, let's assume for a moment that homosexual activity of any kind is a sin. Here is a hypothetical: what if the good news of

Christ as described above is preached and a gay couple responds positively to the message? What should the church that they want to join do?

Here is a splendid example of that. Though it is a different issue, it presents a viable option. In his wonderful book, *Blue Ocean Faith*, author Dave Smeltzer tells a delightful story of a pastor friend of his who was learning to trust the Holy Spirit to do the Spirit's own job. An international arms dealer had an encounter with Christ and became involved in the church that Smeltzer's friend pastored. That pastor became the mentor of the former arms dealer. Here is what happened:

> *One day, the man asked his mentor, "Should I quit smoking?" [The mentor] said, "Well, what's Jesus telling you?" The man took a moment to ask Jesus and then reported back, "He's telling me I should finish smoking the pack I'm on, really enjoy each smoke, and then never smoke again." And that's what the man did. A little later the man asked his mentor, "Should I continue to have sex with my girlfriend or should I stop until I get married?" The church was a conservative church with explicit guidelines on such things, but the pastor stuck to his guns. "What's Jesus saying to you?" The man asked Jesus*

> *and then reported back, "Well, at the
> very least he's saying I should ask her
> to marry me!" And that's what he did.*[93]

When I read Smeltzer's story, the reply that the man heard from Jesus resonated with me, especially the kind, gentle way with which Jesus responded. I thought to myself, "That sounds like my experience with Jesus." This is what Jesus said about himself:

> *Take my yoke upon you. Let me teach
> you, because I am humble and gentle at
> heart, and you will find rest for your
> souls. For my yoke is easy to bear, and
> the burden I give you is light.*[94]

Let's compare what that mentor did with how so many others would have handled it. As for the cigarette issue, most Christians I know (including myself at one time) would offer Bible verses on our bodies being the temple of God, etc. and therefore we are obligated to not smoke. (Of course, the Bible never mentions cigarettes or tobacco, plus those verses are seldom applied to other common unhealthy practices like eating junk food, drinking

---

[93] Smeltzer, Dave, *Blue Ocean Faith*, (Canton, MI: Front Edge Publishing, 2017), p. 43
[94] Matthew 11:29-30. This is also another example of the distinction between John the Baptist's style and that of Jesus. John was "thunder in the desert", both in style and message. Jesus was gentle with a humble demeanor.

soda, getting enough sleep and exercise, or most church potlucks. The scriptural application becomes very selective, but I digress.)

That mentor's advice was brilliant! Encourage the man to talk to Jesus personally, listen, and then follow the instruction.

The second issue of the man sleeping with his girlfriend seems very cut and dry to many Christians. Most believers would declare, "Well, duh! I could have told him that. That is in the Bible!"

My point: we can trust the Holy Spirit to do his job! While in both of those cases Bible verses could have been used accurately, the Spirit of God is greater than the Bible. It also imbues confidence when one knows that the direction comes from the Lord they love and trust, and not simply from someone else's opinion, even if based on scripture.

> *When the Spirit of truth comes, he will guide you into all truth. He will not speak on his own but will tell you what he has heard. He will tell you about the future. He will bring me glory by telling you whatever he receives from me. All that belongs to the Father is mine; this is why I said, 'The Spirit will tell you whatever he receives from me.'* [95]

---

[95] John 16:13-15

But you are not like that, for the Holy One has given you his Spirit, and all of you know the truth... But you have received the Holy Spirit, and he lives within you, so you don't need anyone to teach you what is true. For the Spirit teaches you everything you need to know, and what he teaches is true— it is not a lie. So just as he has taught you, remain in fellowship with Christ. [96]

This is sometimes hard to swallow, especially if one has witnessed another person claim to be "led by the Spirit" but who is just wacky and self-delusional. That is certainly understandable. Unfortunately, it has caused many to slide to the other extreme and declare that we can only trust the written Word – the Bible. Of course, even if one follows *that* path, there are many different perspectives in scripture and no guarantee that being "led" by one's personal reading is any more accurate or balanced. St. Paul, who loved scripture and quoted it throughout his writings, had this to say:

---

[96] 1 John 2:20-27. A note of clarification: some may object and ask, "What about teachers? Didn't God give individuals with teaching ability to the church?" Absolutely. Their function, however, is different. The Greek word for "know" in the above verses is *eido* (pronounced I'-do). It means to know by perception. In this context, the Holy Spirit gives us a holy intuition of what the Lord wants. We "know" something is the right thing to do, even if we do not understand it well. That is where a teacher comes in. A teacher's function is to explain from scripture, reason, and experience what we know intuitively. Both are needed in the appropriate context.

*For all who are **led by the Spirit of God** are children of God.*[97] [Emphasis mine]

The early Christ-followers had minimal access to any scriptures. There was no New Testament and parts of the Hebrew Bible [Old Testament] were confined to expensive scrolls in synagogues. Remember that this era was over 1000 years before the invention of the printing press. Documents had to be hand-copied and were pricy to purchase. People also forget that most early Christ-followers were illiterate, so even if they had access to scrolls, it would do them no good. They could not read!

Even once the New Testament documents were written and began to circulate among various groups, it took centuries for a list of books to coalesce into one volume. Still, there was debate over including a few of them.

The point is that the early Christ-followers could not be "led by the Bible" because there wasn't any, at least in any form like we have today. But--and this is huge--they did have the Holy Spirit. And though they may not have had a 'sophisticated understanding' as we moderns claim to have today, they could still trust the intuitive way in which the Spirit guided them. And the number of Christ-

---

[97] Romans 8:14

followers expanded in numbers and influence throughout the whole Roman empire!

As hard as it is to give up the ego-control of our doctrines and opinions that we believe are biblical, we need to learn to let the Holy Spirit guide us. That is the sign of a child of God, not the ability to pass a Bible-content exam.

We CAN trust the Holy Spirit!

This applies to the issues addressed in this book.

You are not the Holy Spirit.

I am not the Holy Spirit.

Our job: love others without an agenda, demonstrate God's kindness and hospitality, and learn to see all through the eyes of Jesus.

The Holy Spirit can do the rest.

As we end this book, I realize there will be a wide spectrum of reactions. Some will be relieved that what they sensed intuitively is the heart of God and now are able to better contextualize the "clobber" verses. Others may not track with some of my points but hopefully will consider my ideas with a humble and open attitude. I sympathize with them, as I struggled for years with the same fears and concerns. Some will no doubt read this book and become angry, but I honor you for reading it anyway. It is always a challenge to read something that provokes anger, but I have found that in quieter moments later, when one ruminates on what they read, it may still have a positive impact.

Above all, I hope this book will challenge you in growing in love. I close with a short prayer from the New Testament I pray it every day for me and my readers:

> *I pray that from his glorious, unlimited resources he will empower you with inner strength through his Spirit. Then Christ will make his home in your hearts as you trust in him. Your roots will grow down into God's love and keep you strong.* ***And may you have the power to understand, as all God's people should, how wide, how long, how high, and how deep his love is. May you experience the love of Christ, though it is too great to understand fully. Then you will be made complete with all the fullness of life and power that comes from God.***[98] [Emphasis mine]

Amen.

---

[98] Ephesians 3:16-19

APPENDIX – What If Your Child Is Gay?

Congratulations! You have made it through what I hope is a thought-provoking book. I trust it has expanded your perception of our hospitable God and clarified some of the strong (but misapplied) Bible verses concerning this difficult topic. Even if some of my dear readers are not convinced, I hope you are challenged to re-examine your image of our loving heavenly Father as modeled by Jesus.

Though I am specifically addressing the issue of gay family members, these suggestions can be applied to different people groups or situations. Remember, our Father's love toward his creation is as expansive as his universe! Everyone is invited to the party!

For simplicity I will refer to our offspring using the term "child" (even if he or she is an adult). Side note: I have five adult children with their own families and careers. No matter how old they become, they will always be my *kids*. I suspect most good parents share this sentiment.

Below are some practical insights we have learned both by observing others and our own personal experience. Some suggestions address maintaining the right attitudes, while others focus on healthy actions. These thoughts are summaries and applications of various chapters in this book. So here goes…

- God gave your son or daughter to you because he loves you. God does not give defective gifts! Treat your child as God's wonderful precious present that he or she is.
- Your child is not gay because you failed as a parent.
- There is no shame or condemnation from God for receiving and loving your gay child. You have done nothing wrong! In fact, you are following the way of Jesus who loved and received those whom religious leaders considered morally inferior. They did not realize that Jesus modeled our heavenly Father's love.
- Your child needs your unconditional love and support, especially if he or she is "coming out of the closet." Though there are laws against discrimination based on sexual orientation, society can still be rough on the LGBTQ+ community. Your son or daughter needs parents who are a refuge and place of encouragement.
- Accepting your child as gay also means accepting his or her partner.[99] It is a package deal. The partner also can be a wonderful gift from God to your family! My son's husband is a highly educated professional man. He is also

---

[99] Obviously, if a potential partner is abusive or committing criminal acts, a good parent would try to influence their child to make better choices – whether gay or straight.

compassionate, insightful, and a joy to be around. He has become a son to my wife and me, and our family has been enriched by his love and friendship.

- Resist bullies. Sadly, when it comes to homosexuality, many high-profile ministers, local pastors, and other religious leaders express their opinions with extreme authority and confidence, even when unwarranted. If one does not agree with them, that person is not just resisting the speaker but also rebelling against God. If your pastor or favorite Bible teacher has that attitude instead of gentleness and humility, they may be talented - but they are toxic!

> *A servant of the Lord must not quarrel but must be kind to everyone, be able to teach, and be patient with difficult people. Gently instruct those who oppose the truth.*[100]

I am not implying that all who disagree with me are bullies. But if a person is fearful of disapproval from their pastor or spiritual hero, and that fear keeps them from loving

---

[100] 2 Timothy 2:24-25A

their son or daughter, they have been bullied whether they know it or not.

- Don't be surprised by criticism, a loss of respect, de-friending, or even ostracization from members of your faith community, especially if that community is fundamentalist, conservative evangelical, or charismatic. Some communities may seem more "tolerant" of *parents* of gay children and even treat you as a victim for having a gay child. It is how they would feel if your child was a drug addict or a criminal. To them, homosexuality — and especially homosexual relationships (even long-term monogamous ones) — are sin, pure and simple! It's not even a "hate the sin but love the sinner" mentality. It is more of "hate the sin and the sinner but empathize with the sinner's parents."

- If rejected by family members, religious leaders, or friends from your faith community, forgive. And move on. Don't allow bitterness and disillusionment to defeat you. I know this is easier said than done. These are people you care about. Maybe you have invested your time, energy, and resources with them. Perhaps you have been to each other's homes or served in a church together. You love them. And they may love you as well. Though at times the evidence seems otherwise, most Christians are sincere, well-meaning people.

They are simply trying to live out what they have been taught to value by other sincere, well-meaning teachers and leaders. Sadly, those same teachings can be toxic if the fruit of them causes people to resist experiencing the expansive, generous, unreserved, magnanimous love of our heavenly Father. Score: Zeal for doctrinal purity = 1; zeal for love = 0.

A final word about loyalty.

Over the years many of us have been challenged by Jesus' teaching about choosing to follow him over all others, including our family members. His teachings on that subject are still valid today. Some Christian parents have rejected their gay child because they feel they must do so to be loyal to God. But here is an incredible irony — what if following Christ's example of receiving, accepting, and caring for those the religious community rejects (including our own family members) *is* a demonstration of our loyalty and commitment to Jesus?

WWJD — those old bracelets that asked, "What would Jesus do?" will find their answer as we truly follow our Master by adopting his attitudes and practices. So, my friend, accepting your child, co-worker, or neighbor who is gay is not being disloyal to Jesus, no matter what some preachers or churches will try to tell you. Instead, you are following our wonderful savior who perfectly demonstrated our Father's love.

I have decided to follow Jesus… no turning back![101]

ACKNOWLEDGEMENTS

As described in the book, unlearning and re-learning is often a journey. In some cases, the process of "unlearning" can require more time than acquiring new knowledge. For me it took many years. This book is the result of that journey.

The writing was also done during many months of a momentous year – including retirement and my daughter's wedding.

Though for obvious reasons I will not mention names, I am very grateful to those in the LGBTQ+ community who were willing to share with me their struggles, perceptions, and insights. Your perspectives challenged and ultimately helped change my beliefs and attitudes.

Thanks especially to Kaitlyn Light (nee' Brown), my daughter, who is a college English professor and a tough yet thoughtful editor. Her input over five drafts of this book greatly improved the finished product. She managed to balance teaching college classes with tutoring, editing others' books, going to the gym regularly, planning her wedding, marrying, and starting a new life with a wonderful guy.

Chris and Sean, thank you for being *you*! Your intelligence, kindness, character, and courage make us proud and honored that you are a part of our family.

Finally, to Susan Brown. Thanks for agreeing to marry a brash, cocky young man with much more zeal than wisdom and sticking with him for fifty-plus years. You have been not only a stabilizing force through the ups and downs of life but have brought much beauty and grace into our relationship (not to mention five wonderful kids.

ABOUT THE AUTHOR

Dennis Brown is an author, speaker, accomplished musician, and former pastor. He brings a lifetime of experience and years of reflection to this book. He is also the author of *A More Beautiful Faith – Seeing God Through the Eyes of Jesus*. He and his wife live in eastern Tennessee near the Great Smoky Mountains.

For more information about *A More Beautiful Faith*...

Print Version:
ISBN-13: 979-8988575818

Kindle e-book:
A More Beautiful Faith: Seeing God Through the Eyes of Jesus - Kindle edition by Brown, Dennis, Ryskamp, Roger, Brown, Kaitlyn, Dyer, Jody. Religion & Spirituality Kindle eBooks @ Amazon.com.

Make an author happy!
Please leave a review on Amazon.

www.ingramcontent.com/pod-product-compliance
Lightning Source LLC
Chambersburg PA
CBHW060500280326
41933CB00014B/2806